ALONGSIDE

ALONGSIDE

*Reflections on Jesus' Struggles
and how he meets us in Our Struggles*

Daily Readings suitable for Lent,
Advent or any time of the year

HENRY MARTIN

DARTON·LONGMAN+TODD

First published in 2021 by
Darton, Longman and Todd Ltd
1 Spencer Court
140–142 Wandsworth High Street
London SW18 4JJ

Cover image: Two Peasant Women Digging in Field with Snow,
Vincent van Gogh, Oil on canvas 50.0 x 64 cm.
Saint-Remy: March-April, 1890.

ISBN 978-0-232-53464-1

A catalogue record for this book is available from the British Library.

Designed and produced by Judy Linard

Printed and bound in Great Britain by Bell & Bain, Glasgow

'If you would only recognise that life is hard, things would be so much easier for you.'
Louis D. Brandeis

In memory of Anne Martin
31/3/1928 – 1/4/2020

Contents

Introduction: A Jesus who never struggled

It starts with Arnie and Smithy ...

Before the government cuts, the residents used to have evening association in Manchester Prison. This was a time for chatting on the wings, making phone calls and, whenever possible, getting to the gym. There was a group on one wing who asked me, as a Christian chaplain, to run a Bible study group for them. Every Monday night in the period after tea and before bang up at half-past-eight, I would lug my guitar and a bundle of resources up four flights of stairs to their unit.

The only available room had been created by knocking two cells into one. It was essentially the wing's dumping ground for broken equipment, boxes of spare official forms, cleaning materials, some sagging grey filing cabinets, toilet rolls and an unwieldy floor polisher. There were two small arched windows each with five bars. These were placed higher than in a conventional room. Their purpose was solely to let in light not provide a view.

Amid the detritus, sitting on some scruffy seats a group of us met to sing, pray, read and learn together. It was the least church-like space I could imagine, but conversely the setting for some of the most church-like experiences of my life.

I need to change names here as the identities of the group members should be protected.

Arnie was a quiet, stout, smiling man. He attended

the group cheerfully every week and never missed Sunday services. He carried that unspoken aura of one who should not be crossed, not because he might be violent, or had friends who could weigh in on his behalf, there was simply something about Arnie that people respected. He was also unusual in a jail full of 'innocent' men, in that he owned his crime and complied fully with every rehabilitation course going.

One winter's evening, just before the start of Lent, I had prepared some questions about Jesus' temptations. The most fascinating conversation followed.

It came down to Arnie and Smithy. Smithy was also a chapel regular, but had never shown much interest in church on the outside. Since coming in, he had read voraciously and knew his way around the Bible better than most.

Smithy: So when Jesus was tempted, he must have really wanted what was on offer?

Arnie: No. Absolutely not. Jesus never wanted anything that was wrong.

Smithy: But if he didn't want any bread, how were the stones any temptation?

Arnie: Because it was the devil. Whatever the devil wants to give is always wrong and therefore always temptation.

Smithy: But if he didn't crave the bread … if he wasn't hungry, if his body wasn't screaming with every fibre in it for some food, then he wasn't tempted. It's easy to say 'no' to something you don't deeply want.

I did not mention it earlier, but all the prisoners on this wing were in for sexual offences and as such were likely to have strong feelings about the nature of temptation.

Arnie: Jesus did not want anything bad. Ever. He is Jesus. He is God's own Son and God is good.

Smithy: But when the devil showed him all the world and he could have it all. Didn't he feel the pull of that? He could complete his mission without the cross ... without any pain or suffering.

Arnie: Jesus only wanted to do the right thing. There is no way he would have considered anything, not for even a moment if one of the conditions was worshipping the devil.

Smithy: Forget the devil for the moment. Look at the prize before him. Wouldn't he have been drawn to it ... desired it ... yearned for it? Okay, I don't get why jumping of a building was so attractive to him, but getting bread from stones and gaining power over the whole world ... surely he wanted that?

Arnie: You say, 'forget the devil', but you can't forget the devil. Not even for a moment. The devil was right there in front of him. You can't tell me and I'm not having it that Jesus would have seriously considered anything the devil offered him. Aren't you forgetting, he is the Son of God?

As much as I respected Arnie, I was with Smithy. Arnie's Jesus was a rock solid, immovable good 'un, the ultimate good 'un who unlike Arnie had no risk of ever falling for temptation. I appreciated why Arnie might need that certainty, given his past. However, on this issue I remained with Smithy. The greater Jesus' ease at dismissing, the less his struggle, the less his victory and the less help he can be to us now.

How many other things were difficult for Jesus? There are several stories in the Gospels where he appears rattled. This book seeks to explore some of these, from the annoyances of bickering disciples, to the hassles of uncomprehending crowds, through his many disputes with his co-religionists until we finally arrive at his greatest struggle, his moment of final decision in the garden of Gethsemane.

I ended the evening worried that Arnie's Jesus could never understand Arnie's struggles. His Jesus would be always upfront, offering a shining example to lead him on but could never get alongside him and meet him *in* his struggles. In terms of St Patrick's Breastplate Arnie was entirely au fait with 'Christ before me' but much less so with 'Christ be with me' and certainly not when it came to Christ sharing his struggles.

Arnie was always on safer ground talking about his love for God's creation. From the centre of Manchester, you cannot see many stars even on a clear night, but Arnie loved the times when the angles lined up and from his bunk he could see the moon, through his too-high window. The moon spoke to him of the beauty of God's creation and when he saw it, it brought to him also all the forests, mountains, glaciers, deserts, oceans and wildlife of our own planet … and he felt grateful to God.

Perhaps this book will result in a long overdue and implausibly protracted reply to Arnie. If he ever reads it I hope he finds that there is good news, encouragement and some seriously worthwhile help to be found in a Jesus who struggled then and who can be alongside us in our struggles now.

Life free from struggle

Once upon a time there was a sermon illustration … which if not fully true, ought to be true. It begins with a preacher's child who was a kindly soul with a passion for natural history. She had found a chrysalis and watched with great excitement as it started to twitch with emerging life. It cracked to reveal a moth whose slow egress was painful to watch. It bucked, it jerked and it strained but made such little progress that she could see little prospect of it ever breaking free from its once protective shell. She saw a way to help. She took a scalpel and made some delicate cuts, taking great care not to touch the animal with the blade. The moth was soon out but it never flew. Its wings had been denied the struggle that would have grown the muscles required for flight. What the child had failed to understand was this: struggle is not a block to life rather it is a necessity. In rescuing the moth, her intended kindness had quite literally spoilt it.

Jesus understands our human need to struggle, to wrestle and engage. He weaves his truths into the fabric of stories rather than spoon-feeding them directly to his listeners. They have to enter into his parables and squeeze, mine, chew, contemplate, compare and reflect and only then, only once they are fully inhabiting his narratives, does his wisdom start to reveal itself. The struggle is an integral part of the lesson. Jesus might almost have said, 'If I give you a straight answer, I will rob you of your chance of ever learning it.' (My words not his.)

We would prefer the shortcut. We have perverted the word 'comfort'. To us it now conjures snuggling under freshly laundered bedding, cuddling a snoozing puppy, with a warm drink beside us while a hard rain beats against the windowpanes. We are secure and all is at peace. Comfort's original meaning is quite some distance from this. Literally 'fort' derives from the Latin *fortis* meaning 'strong'. The prefix 'com' (and its variations 'co' and 'con') imply adding to, bringing together or joining with. When Isaiah relays God's message,

'Comfort, comfort my people says your God ...'[1]

he envisions God making us strong in a time of struggle, rather than wrapping us in a duvet (or to use their American name, a 'comforter'). 'Comfort' is as much a call to engage, as a call to rest.

[1] Isaiah 40:1.

The name 'Israel' means struggle or contention. It was first given to Jacob, after he had wrestled with God at Peniel.[2] The fact that his descendant Jesus also struggled should not come as a surprise. To Arnie this notion verged on heresy but it is outside the Bible, in the *apocryphal* not in the canonical Gospels that Jesus dodges life's struggles and even death. According to the Second Treatise of the Great Seth, the man on the cross who took the vinegar and gall was not Jesus.

'It was another upon Whom they placed the crown of thorns. But I was rejoicing in the height over all the wealth of the archons and the offspring of their error, of their empty glory. And I was laughing at their ignorance.'[3]

This is not the Jesus of the four Gospels. He would not slink away, snidely laughing at a mistake which left another to die in agony.

The real Jesus' life was by no means struggle-free. If like him, we trace our spiritual ancestry back to Jacob, we should not expect exemption from struggles in our lives. They are integral to our learning, thriving, believing and living.

Caution, mind the cultural gap

Jesus' struggles are revealed to us almost entirely through his words. He gives many unexpectedly sharp replies and makes some alarmingly stark comments which, even after all mitigating factors have been taken into account, seem born of frustration and struggle.

Jesus' words must never be understood solely as they appear in our twenty-first-century minds. Being over-literal and shunning his cultural context will lead us to any number of dangerous things done supposedly in his name, such as:

[2] Genesis 32:28.
[3] From *The Second Treatise of the Great Seth*, translated by Roger A. Bullard and Joseph A. Gibbons.

hating our parents, choosing church duties over attending our dad's funeral or gouging out our own eyes.

Cultural context is everything. I first came to the north of England as a student. I found a summer job collecting weekly insurance payments on a large housing estate in the south of Leeds. The first week went well but during the second I got confused and entered the wrong figures into the wrong columns of the wrong book. This meant that my manager had a bag of coins and a book of figures that bore no relation to each other. He called me into his office. He said,

'You're a little bugger you are!'

I was mortified. I knew I had messed up but clearly this was far worse than I had imagined. Was I going to lose my job? Would I be fined the shortfall if the books did not balance?

But my manager was smiling. He had just sworn at me but he was still smiling. And only his words, not his voice had been angry. Apparently it could all be sorted out; it would just take time and effort and for that I was a 'little bugger'.

A while later I discovered that in Leeds, calling someone a 'bugger' and only a little one, carries none of the weight I had supposed. Back at home in 1970s and 1980s Essex I had only heard it used in serious anger. In Yorkshire it meant little more than a silly chump.

In 2000 I returned to the North, this time as an ordained member of the clergy. On my first funeral visit I asked a grieving man what his father had been like. He smiled and shrugged,

'Oh he was all right. He was a good person. He never murdered anyone.'

Okay, this is not what he said but rather what I heard. At the time I was trying to stop my jaw from dropping too far, thinking,

'Wow! He's setting a very low base line for his definition of a good person.'

Of course, what he actually said was,

'He never *mithered* anyone.'

But I had never heard this word before and so my southern-tuned ears, turned it into something quite different.

I remind myself of these little episodes when I read the Gospels, especially in those awkward times when Jesus comes across as unnecessarily grumpy. The distance from Essex to the North of England may be further in cultural difference than it is in miles. I now sit in Manchester, over 3000 miles from the Holy Land, at a 2000 year remove from the events of Jesus' earthly life. I have grown up in a culture that would be at times confusing if not entirely alien to Simon Peter and Mary Magdalene. This means that as I read the words of Jesus, I can never understand everything about their context.

I am further debilitated by such a deep reliance on words alone. The cliché goes that 93 per cent of communication is non-verbal. Whatever the exact figure, I am clearly missing out. I have no ability, beyond imagination, to hear Jesus' tone of voice or see his facial expressions. There are some scholars who can help me identify some but not all the cultural shorthands he uses. Jokes in particular do not travel well. I imagine Jesus as a humorous wordsmith who enjoys irony, much of which has been lost in transit across culture and through time.

Translation is also key. Jesus says something and one version of the Bible records this as a mere statement while another renders it as a barked insult. For example, when Peter does not understand a parable he asks for clarification. [4] In the NRSV Jesus replies to Peter with the neutral:

'Are you also still without understanding?'

This is very different in tone from the NIV's caustic,

'Are you still so dull?'

This latter sends me straight back to the worst of my schoolteachers who took all requests for clarification as

[4] Matthew 15:15.

criticism of their ability and then retaliated by mocking their pupils' intelligence. I expect better from Jesus. I hope that as a good teacher, he would check for understanding and deal patiently with those lagging behind. When, as now, I am confronted by conflicting translations I wish I had paid more attention in my New Testament Greek classes. As I am unable to turn back the clock, I have decided to stick with the anglicized version of the NRSV in this book.

The outward signs of inner conflict

I approached a psychiatrist friend with a question. He naturally sees many people in different stages of turmoil. I asked him what signs would alert him that a patient is undergoing some sort of internal struggle. He answered with a list of possibilities:

- Extreme or 'jarring' language
- Withdrawal from normal communication
- Avoiding eye contact
- Extreme eye contact
- Contorted facial expressions
- Abrupt changes in mood
- Unexpected or inappropriate responses to non-threatening situations
- Being in a state of distraction or easily being distracted
- Rapid development of anxiety and in extreme cases psychosis.

We struggle to find all of these in Jesus, not necessarily because they did not exist, but more because we only have a written record of his life. With just his words and the occasional reference to a gesture to go on, we need to proceed with a measure of caution and a careful exercise in imagination. Even so, Jesus' words surely reveal times when he is struggling or conflicted. Why else would he call someone a 'whitewashed tomb', beautiful on the outside, but inside full of dead bones and filth?[5] By anyone's standards this is extremely offensive and certainly not the product of a happy mind-set.

It is comments like this that I wish to investigate further in this book. If nothing else, we might know Jesus a little better by the end. I am optimistic of more. I want to explore how and why Jesus struggled. I hope to find a decent answer for Arnie and gain some insights into how Jesus can draw alongside him, and us, in whatever struggles we face today.

How and when to use this book

This book is for any time of the year; our struggles are not regulated by the calendar. However many seek something meaningful to read during Advent and Lent and so at the end of each of the six parts I have added some extra questions for these seasons. I hope these will be especially useful to those who study this book as part of a group, whether online or in person.

It has been designed as a six-week read, with a reflection for each day from Monday to Friday, followed by a concluding thought and some questions which can be read over Saturday and Sunday, along with the next introduction .

Advent readers will find too many reflections for one each day and so might like to skip a whole chapter or alternatively keep on reading into the New Year and Epiphany. There is a special reflection which can be read on or near Christmas Day (see p. 234 and appendix 1 on p. 251 for a possible Advent reading plan.)

Advent is a complicated season since its length varies. Advent Sunday can fall as early as 27 November and as late as 3 December, so Advent books risk either being too long, requiring the reader to double up on some days, or too short if they begin like Advent calendars on 1 December. I have yet to find a perfect solution to this.

---

[5] Matthew 23:27.

Lent is easier despite the changeable date of Ash Wednesday, as it is always a fixed length. Lenten readers will find the material fits the season if they begin with the introduction from Ash Wednesday to the first Saturday and then take a week to read each of the six chapters, using the weekends for the concluding thought and questions (or for catching up on the odd missed day). There is a final reflection which can be read on Easter Sunday (see p. 237 and appendix 2 on p. 252 for a possible Lent reading plan.)

Introduction: A Jesus who never struggled

Questions for any time of year

1. Before you proceed much further with this book, with whom do you agree more, Arnie or Smithy?
   a. Did Jesus struggle or did he rise above his difficulties?
   b. Did Jesus crave and yearn for bread or did he dismiss such thoughts with ease, as he saw their origin?

2. And without looking ahead at the chapter titles, write a list of all the things you think Jesus might have found difficult.

3. And then write a second list of stressful things that bizarrely did not bother him at all.

4. Have you ever been shocked by something Jesus said that sounded uncharacteristically harsh?

5. Have you ever had a sense of Jesus being alongside you in your struggles?
   a. If so would you be able to describe this experience to someone else?
   b. If not, what might we expect to find from Jesus?

6. Thinking of the child and the chrysalis:
   a. Has anyone ever spared you a struggle but at the same time, deprived you of an opportunity to grow?
   b. Have you ever removed a struggle from someone kindly but inadvisably?
   c. How dangerous is kindness without wisdom?

Introduction: A Jesus who never struggled

Questions for Advent

1. How will Jesus feature in your plans for this coming Christmas? At which points in your seasonal busy-ness are you most likely to lose sight of Jesus alongside you?

2. Where do you expect to find joy and where do you anticipate struggles this Advent?

3. In this season of darkening nights[6] what kind of 'comfort' do you seek from God?

4. Will there be times of stillness this Advent?
   a. How will you create them?
   b. How will you guard them?

5. Imagine you could start with a blank sheet, forgetting all that we usually do around December 25th, and design an annual celebration for the birth of Jesus:
   a. What would it look like?
   b. How long would it last? A day? A week? Twelve days? Longer?
   c. What would you consider when setting your budget?
   d. What aspects of Jesus' personality would you seek to reflect in your plans?
   e. How would you tailor your celebrations to bring him delight on his birthday?

---

[6] At least for those reading this book in the northern hemisphere.

Introduction: A Jesus who never struggled

Questions for Lent

1. Do you usually plan Lent or do you take it as it comes? Do you consider previous Lents? Or do you start each from scratch?
    a. Do you devise new activities and disciplines or do you expand on what has worked well in the past?
    b. Will your focus be on what you are giving up or taking up?

2. Will there be times of stillness this Lent?
    a. How will you create them?
    b. How will you guard them?

3. If you could ask Jesus just one question (and receive a straight answer) what would you ask him about his forty days and nights in the wilderness?

4. Jesus quoted the scriptures at each point of his temptation. What role do the scriptures play in your struggles and everyday life?

5. Imagine you could start with a blank sheet, forgetting all we usually do around Easter and design an annual event to recall the passion of Jesus and celebrate his resurrection:
    a. What would it look like?
    b. How long would it last? A day? A week? Longer?
    c. What would you consider when setting your budget?
    d. What aspects of Jesus' story would you seek to highlight in your plans?
    e. Which of his teachings would be at the forefront of your mind when planning for his resurrection?

PART ONE

Jesus struggled with his family

Introduction – Jesus struggled with his family

Jesus struggles with his family and they struggle with him. They are family together and family life can be difficult.

We see family tensions building as the eldest child sets himself up as a healer, a Sabbath breaker and exorcist. His family plan an intervention, when he and his auspicious number of disciples cannot move without getting mobbed. Mark records,

> When his family heard it, they went out to restrain him, for people were saying, 'He has gone out of his mind.'[7]

Many try to restrain Jesus, alongside his own family members. None fare well; not his disciples, the crowds or the Pharisees. When restraint finally comes, it is at the hands of the Romans and at a time of Jesus' own choosing.

But we are getting ahead of ourselves, so back to his family and his struggles with them ...

---

[7] Mark 3:21.

Day 1: Jesus struggled with his family but maybe not so much when he was small

And Jesus increased in wisdom and in years and in divine and human favour. *Luke 2:52*

I had an epiphany one afternoon in the prison chapel. I had taken one of the residents there to light a candle. It was the first anniversary of his mother's death. After he had lit his candle and said 'Amen' to our prayers he showed no signs of wanting to return to his wing, so I started asking him about his life. He told me how his mum had gone back to drugs after his brother was born. He had been just three at the time. What followed was a catalogue of abuses from a procession of her boyfriends who posed as step-fathers. He was in many ways, the adult in his family: a burden of responsibility that no child should ever be required to shoulder.

Sadly, I had heard this sort of thing all too often but on this day a penny dropped. Perhaps it was his matter of fact tone or maybe his evident grief for the mother whom he loved, despite the poor start she had given him in life or maybe there was some unconnected conversation I had recently had with my own parents; from wherever it came, a realisation hit me like a sledgehammer.

I too could trot out a list of complaints about my upbringing, the times when was I was misunderstood, left without guidance, bruised by arguments and so on. My epiphany on that day brought an understanding of the space such gripes occupied in my wider script. They are odd lines, small paragraphs and brief footnotes amongst huge volumes of everyday stability, the kind of care and routine that makes for dull reading and is therefore all too easy to overlook. My woes are not irrelevant but they must be seen in context.

Unlike me this poor fellow had many more woes and far less padding in between. Regular mealtimes, school runs, parents at parent teacher meetings, fixed bedtimes, shoes that fit, help with homework, clear rules, arbitration in sibling rivalry, aspirations, positive role models, a clean home and no shortage of everyday affection are unremarkable for those who know nothing else. Their familiarity renders them nearly invisible. For me, to finally see their immensity, I needed to meet this young man who had enjoyed no such childhood 'dullness' in which his adult future could quietly grow. Therapists will still get their well-deserved shilling from me; my issues did not evaporate following this conversation but they had found a new context. A penny had dropped further and deeper than before.

I am guessing that an eye-witness observer of Jesus' family could likewise fill several volumes with accounts of similar unremarkable kindness. Maybe if Jesus had been born into the Instagram generation we would be blessed with much more. Some of my friends' children cannot put on a new t-shirt without another picture of them appearing on timelines across the globe. As it is, Jesus was born long before any of this was imaginable and we have almost nothing of his childhood on record. There are stories from beyond the Bible, in the Apocrypha of the young Jesus moulding clay birds and breathing life into them. I am choosing to discount these, as they were written so long after the canonical Gospels and conjuring live birds reminds me more of Hermione Granger than Jesus of Nazareth.

What do we know? Are his younger days filled with

struggles? Matthew recounts how, as a baby, Jesus becomes an immigrant refugee when his parents take him to Egypt, fleeing the madness of King Herod.[8] We can only speculate whether this episode leaves any lasting trauma in his developing mind. On their return home, the family settles in Nazareth, creating the home where Jesus matures, and into which his siblings are born. The Gospels and other historical sources tell us that his land is occupied by the Romans and squeezed by their exorbitant taxes. There is no record of violence in his early years, although rumours of war are ever present, and up in the hills bands of resistance fighters plot the occupation's end. We therefore can assume that the circumstances around his young life, though far from ideal are also not too turbulent.

We know nothing more apart from the one incident when Jesus gets left behind in the Temple. The struggles here belong more to Mary and Joseph than to their precocious eldest, who answers their panic with confident insouciance:

'Why were you searching for me? Did you not know that I must be in my Father's house?'[9]

In my mind this is delivered much as a modern twelve-year-old would say, 'Well, duh?'

Beyond this there is just silence. Arguments from silence are always tricky but as the cliché goes, no news is good news. This leads me to my hunch that Jesus grows up surrounded by the nurturing routines of dull stability and everyday kindness, whose combined value cannot be underestimated

Jesus suffers a bereavement, but we have no idea when this comes. Joseph disappears from the narrative. He is alive when Jesus is twelve but that is the last time we hear of him. Most guess that he dies before Jesus starts his public ministry but how the two get along and how Jesus reacts to his death remains unknown. Brian Sibley has written a wonderful fable

[8] Matthew 2:13-15.
[9] Luke 2:49.

imaginatively filling some of these gaps, pondering a warm positive relationship between the two.[10]

We might find, if we wish, Joseph's influence in his son's teachings about fathers; Jesus certainly understood that fathers should be kind[11] and that children should embrace their duties to their parents.[12] Again we know too little to guess how much can be attributed to his experiences of Joseph. All we can say that it is fairly likely that Jesus experienced grief in his young life.

It is undeniable that Jesus' interactions with his family were not always cordial. The Gospels mostly record the awkward encounters. Reflections on these will fill the next few pages but they must not be divorced from the wider, unseen context of security, kindness and dull routine.

Despite the assurances of the Christmas carol,[13] Jesus is our childhood's pattern only in the very broadest sense, in that he was born and reached adulthood. There are zero firm details about how, 'day by day, like us he grew'. 'Tears and smiles' are reasonable guesses despite another carol's insistence that even as a waking baby 'no crying he makes'.[14] There are no stories of his teething, his playing, his schooling, his growing pains or how he fared during the storms of adolescence.

Mel Gibson invents a scene in which Jesus as a boy trips over and Mary rushes to comfort him.[15] Then he contrasts this with her inability to aid him, as he falls on the road to Golgotha. This certainly ramps up the pathos in his gory film and might even contain some truth. He creates further scenes including one in which Jesus invents the modern upright dining chair. This merely demonstrates the dangers of too much anachronistic speculation.

[10] Brian Sibley, *Joseph and the Three Gifts* (Darton, Longman and Todd, 2019).
[11] Luke 15:11-32.
[12] Matthew 15:5-6.
[13] 'Once in Royal David's City', Cecil Frances Alexander, 1848.
[14] 'Away In A Manger', author unknown.
[15] *The Passion of the Christ*, Newmarket Films, directed by Mel Gibson 2004.

Alongside us

There is not much here to aid those who struggle with a truly awful childhood. This is not to say Jesus is unable draw alongside them but there is no neat collection of tales from which we can easily conclude, *Jesus can meet you in your struggles because as you can see, he went through pretty much the same.*

For the rest of us, our struggle might simply be one of gaining perspective. I am quite staggered by how long it took me to assemble many fragmentary pages of gripes whilst not seeing my volumes of 'dull' stability. I remain fascinated with this awkward period and given the lack of stories about the younger Jesus, I find solace in autobiographies.[16] If nothing else, they reassure me that I was not the only teenager whose mammoth outrage at minor injustices occluded almost everything else.

I have taken liberties with the Church of England's collect for Mothering Sunday:

> God of compassion,
> whose Son Jesus Christ, the child of Mary,
> shared the life of a home in Nazareth,
> and somehow navigated
> those struggles of childhood and adolescence
> common to the whole human family:
> aid our remembrances of sorrows and joys
> that we may find your wider perspective
> and so finally appreciate the many kindnesses
> that unresolved pain or over-familiarity,
> might otherwise render invisible. **AMEN**.

---

[16] My favourite being Stephen Fry's *Moab is My Washpot* (Random House, 1997).

Day 2: Jesus struggled with his family when they failed to forget how he was once a kid

'Is not this the carpenter, the son of Mary and brother of James and Joses and Judas and Simon, and are not his sisters here with us?' And they took offence at him. *Mark 6:3*

There is a type of person – let's call them A – who delights in saying things like,

A: Look at you now you're all grown up, but it only seems like yesterday when you were running across the park with no trousers or pants on.

B: So you say … every time I come back home and we meet. And as I always reply … I was only three at the time. I'm a doctor now.

A: Well to me it's like yesterday. To me you'll always be that little streaker.

I am entirely with B here if A's subtext is, 'you clearly think you're so high and mighty and it's my duty is to bring you back down to earth.' B's point is, 'Yes once, many years ago I *was* a child and *now* I'm an adult.'

A grates on my nerves but that does not explain my

annoying urge to remind my niece at every major stage in her life (going to secondary school, passing her driving test, getting her first tattoo) about how I saw her within half an hour of her birth and how funny she looked with her hair sticking up. Maybe becoming an A is an inevitable (if unattractive) part of growing older.

I might be making a bit of stretch here by including this thought in the chapter about Jesus' struggles with his family. The people speaking in Mark's verse are not his direct family but rather those among whom Jesus grows up. These are the 'village' from the proverb 'it takes a village to raise a child,' who earlier declare, 'He has gone out of his mind', prompting his family to plan an intervention and restrain him.[17] I have taken their words as part and parcel of the general attitude that meets him when he returns to his family home in Nazareth.

For all they love us, family, both biological and village, will at times hold us back. Possibly they fear that our growing up will entail a growing away, for which they are not ready. They hold a devastating repository of memories from our younger days. Mercifully, for my generation these exist only as stories. Future fifty-year-olds will have to live with online video footage of their seventeen-year-old selves too drunk to carry their pint whilst teetering towards a ditch. But for me and all who came before, including Jesus, our childhood antics exist as an oral tradition maintained by that small circle of family and neighbours.

This can make adult conversation nigh on impossible with certain family members especially if, as Jesus did, you have some controversial things to say. An easy way to defend against an unwelcome challenge is to belittle the challenger; even the mightiest have families equipped with an arsenal of stories to deploy in such circumstances.

Maybe we should not be surprised that Jesus performs fewer signs among those who had seen him grow up. His

[17] Mark 3:21.

home audience in Nazareth are delighted at first when he reads in the synagogue,[18] but then he continues with his own commentary. The more he speaks the less they like him and they switch from lionising to lynching with alarming speed. Are they annoyed because he refuses to repeat the repertoire of miracles that went down so well in nearby Capernaum? Or do they resent being 'educated' by an upstart who, only yesterday was just a snotty toddler?

Jesus seeks his own safety and puts some distance between himself and those who cannot cope with his emerging identity or as Luke puts it, '… he passed through the midst of them and went on his way.'[19]

Alongside us

It is good to know that Jesus understands how conflicted family relationships can become, as people grow. A happy family is never a static thing. We are constantly renegotiating our positions. Worrying about the future or grieving too deeply for 'the-good-old-days-when-everything-was-as-it-should-be' will certainly tarnish whatever happens today.

Jesus also understands that the people who witness our childhood, can be restricting. There are reasons why he refuses them some of things that he willingly offers to strangers. Some of these are hard to articulate and there is a fine line between resentful compliance and rude rejection. Somehow Jesus walks his version of this tightrope and can draw alongside us as we face ours. He has no direct experience of the gut-wrenches of parenthood, especially when it comes to allowing children to find their own wings, but his parable of the Waiting Father (or 'the Prodigal Son' as we call it)[20] is evidence that he also walks that path, at least in his imagination.

All of us have episodes in our pasts that we would love

[18] Luke 4:16-30.
[19] Luke 4:30.
[20] Luke 15:11-32.

to leave there. These can range from a hair-dying disaster in our 'self-discovery phase' to far more serious, even criminal acts. Some people can shake free from these, some make one mistake that burdens them for life, others find in later life a long-buried incident returns to haunt them. Perhaps the best we can do within our families is to allow each other to move on, forgiving past hurts and resisting their resurrection, even when we want to score a point in an argument. It boils down to this; we do well to treat others, even our family members, as we would like to be treated ourselves.

Those escaping abuse might find solace in Jesus' companionship, since he, too, refuses to stay with people who intend him harm.

Loving God awaken us to our outdated restrictions,
and lead us to face our wrongful restricting.
Wise Teacher guide us into your way of protesting,
and school us in your way of listening.
Holy Reconciler lead us into all truth,
and give us the courage to bear it well. **AMEN**

Day 3: Jesus struggled with his family when they demanded his attendance

Who is my mother, and who are my brothers?'
And pointing to his disciples, he said, 'Here are my
mother and my brothers!'
Matthew 12:48b-49

Christmas is not even the Marmite of the seasons. At least with Marmite, people are cleanly divided into two camps, 'love it' or 'loathe it'. Christmas can induce both passions within the same person at the same time. At best, as the crown of the year, it is the time for mutual appreciation and delightful familial generosity. At worst, it throws the harshest spotlight on otherwise hidden dysfunctions.

Take Christmas dinner. Many families have lost the habit of sharing a table and for most of the year will eat randomly, sometimes in pairs or threes but rarely all together and it is even less likely to find everyone eating the same thing. Often the family cook creates a personalised menu for each diner, that might be enjoyed at a table or in front of the telly or taken off to a bedroom. Then comes Christmas Day and we fall prey to a vision of perfection; the whole family seated and laughing around a laden table as if in a Norman Rockwell painting.[21] Phones and tablets are replaced by smiles and paper hats. Crackers are pulled

[21] See Rockwell's 1942 painting *Freedom From Want*.

and sprouts rejoiced over, in a hubbub of cheerful conversation.

The reality for many is very far from the expectation. It is not that we do not like each other or that we find we are terrible people once our devices are switched off. It is more that family is an art, a continually evolving exercise in negotiation and an ongoing process of readjusting expectations. This is a highly complex game and imagining we can suddenly switch gear from 'idle' to 'full-throttle' at Christmas, is akin to leaping straight from the sofa into a full marathon with no prior training. Muscles get pulled, tendons strained, old injuries flare up and we hit 'the wall' long before the cheese and biscuits finishing line.

The truth is, families are difficult. We evolve faster than those closest to us would like. If we do not regularly share a table with our nearest and dearest, we come as those unaware of how we have become strangers. Also when we gather together at holiday times, an invisible siren calls us to revert to our traditional roles. Adults can find themselves unconsciously reprising their childhood statuses as family jokers, peacemakers, rebels or trouble-stirrers, despite having relinquished these long ago in every other walk of life.

So much for the 'loathe it' aspect of Christmas; the very fact we keep on attempting to attain the Rockwell vision testifies to our undeniable 'love it'.

While I was working in prison, it became starkly clear how important family is to those denied daily access to their loved ones. Visits are essential. Chaplains are often called upon when regular contact goes awry. Even for the severely dysfunctional, family remains integral. I met some men whose behaviour declared they had nothing to lose but even the most foul-mouthed, urine-throwing, contempt-dripping, repeat-offending, nuisance-making of them, had someone on the outside who had not fully closed the door on them … and 99 times out of 100 that person was a family member.

Family is always family and there is something unbelievably

resilient about the ties that bind us together. We choose our friends but we are stuck with our families, for better or for worse. Wherever our achievements have landed us, family ties always guarantee privileged access between us.

So what is happening when Jesus' wanderings bring him back to his childhood stomping ground and Mary, his sisters and brothers all troop out expecting a family reunion? Maybe they are already feeling snubbed since he has not called on them first? If so they are further snubbed when he refuses to come out to meet them. He is in the middle of an overcrowded house yet somehow they manage to get word through to him. His response, when relayed back to them, is far from encouraging.

Who is my mother, and who are my brothers?' And pointing to his disciples, he said, 'Here are my mother and my brothers!' [22]

They find he has repositioned them. They, his childhood family are now just one part of his much wider family. In fact *anyone* who is obedient to God has as much call on his time as Mary, his brothers and his sisters. This has got to hurt them, at least as much as it might delight others with ears to hear. We in turn, find ourselves asking why Jesus would choose to be so blunt?

Again we are back in the uncertain realms of guesswork. Maybe Jesus feels that to respond to their call would be to confirm their rights to his time; rights that have changed since he left home. Do they come with expectations about the duties of eldest sons? Maybe Jesus feels that acceding to the role they *define* would only *confine* him. Maybe he is suspicious of an attempt to rope him back into whatever position he held in his junior years: family joker, rebel or peacemaker (but hopefully not trouble-stirrer). This is a tantalising game for us to play but ultimately it can only ever be a guessing game.

[22] Matthew 12:48b-49.

Alongside us

It is less important that we know exactly *why* Jesus objects to this call from his family, than it is for us to see that he *did* object. Clearly there was some sort of struggle here. Jesus' family dynamics are hardly likely to match ours. How many of us have questioned a sibling's ability to turn water into wine? It is enough to know that the grown-up Jesus struggles with unwelcome expectations from his family.

However loving or not our families may be, we too will have awkward moments when we feel pressurised to behave in a certain way, because someone else has assigned that role to us. The transition from childhood to adult roles is never without friction, especially in families and even more so at Christmas.

In such times Jesus can draw alongside us, because he is familiar with these sort of struggles since he has walked his own version of this path before us.

Loving Jesus,
in our family lives,
help us to draw and to maintain fair boundaries,
encourage us to seek the softest borders possible,
remind us to negotiate,
to respect,
to adapt as times and people change,
so that together we may live,
true to your calling. **AMEN**

Day 4: Jesus struggled with his family but family still matters

Is there anyone among you who, if your child asks for a fish, will give a snake instead of a fish? Or if the child asks for an egg, will give a scorpion? If you then, who are evil, know how to give good gifts to your children, how much more will the heavenly Father give the Holy Spirit to those who ask him!'

Luke 11:11-13

Jesus *never* said:

'Your family will always be a ton of unnecessary hassle
AND they'll be toxic,
AND they'll utterly oppose all God's plans for you,
AND totally mess up your holy discipleship.
So if you really love God, you MUST cut all ties with them.'

Of course Jesus never said this or anything approaching this but some cult leaders have nevertheless put similar words into his mouth. They find their recruits are so much more pliable (and so much more generous) once separated from their families. I can see how they pull this trick; just as the Gospels omit the everyday stories of Jesus' childhood they also fail to record any of his happy family get-togethers. Instead they focus on some notably awkward occasions when Jesus says things, which taken out of their moment, might lead us to

43

completely discard our families in the noble pursuit of God's kingdom. Cult leaders hope so. Sensible reading demands otherwise.

Jesus expects fathers, even bad ones, to provide for their children. Family is a good thing, even for selfish and greedy people. Are there any fathers so bad that they would give their hungry children scorpions instead of eggs or snakes instead of fish?[23] Sadly, our prisons tell us 'yes'; they house a small number of fathers who have given terrible injuries to their children. They are, however, the exception. Parents in general, however fallible, infuriating, misguided, prejudiced, unaware or just plain stupid, share this bottom line; they desire good things for their children.

We can see how much Jesus is in favour of families on several occasions:

(i) *when the Pharisees try to dodge their duties to their parents*

We witness Jesus railing against an anti-family trick of the Pharisees.[24] Early on in his ministry a group of them travel all the way from Jerusalem to Galilee to investigate him. On arrival, their opening gambit is a dig at his disciples for not washing their hands properly before meals. Jesus counters this with a stinging criticism. He accuses them of twisting scripture to circumvent the duties of adult children to aged parents. They propose that everything they owe is now going to be given to God, as if kindness to parents and love for God are mutually exclusive. Jesus declares that they 'make void the word of God', before slamming them with some choice words from Isaiah. Jesus is overtly clear that family duties are sacred and moreover using God-talk to subvert them, is obscene.

(ii) *when a man tries to recruit him in a feud*

Jesus does not sanction the splitting up of families for one member's personal gain. A man who requests his help in an

---

[23] Luke 11:11-13.
[24] Matthew 15:1-9.

inheritance feud against his brother, is rewarded with both a warning and a parable about the folly of greed. [25] Family is more important than the love of money.

(iii) when he teaches, using positive images of family life
Jesus expects family to be a place of forgiveness and refuge. The extraordinary thing about the parable of the prodigal son [26] is the extravagance of the father's love, which far surpasses normal goodness. The crimes of the younger son (wishing his father were dead already[27]) and of the elder (treating him like a slave driver and publicly refusing his invitation to come home) so transgress the expected order that to many exclusion would be justified. Jesus' parable points to divine love being even greater than that of the most loving earthly parent. He leads his audience to this from a shared starting point, that families are expected to be good, tolerant, accepting and forgiving.

(iv) when he speaks about protective relationships
Jesus looks out at the troubled city of Jerusalem and wishes he could be, as a chicken to them.[28] He pictures a mother hen gathering her vulnerable young under her protective wings and he sees himself in her. He pities the lost of the city and longs to mother and shelter not only them, but all of God's wayward children. In saying this, he affirms his expectation that family relationships should be protective.

So given all this, what do we do with those awkward moments when Jesus tells his disciples to hate their parents,[29] ignore their funerals [30] and not bother to tell them about their

---

[25] Luke 12:13-21.

[26] Luke 15:11-32.

[27] See pages 161-9 Chapter 7, 'Exegesis of Luke 15' in *Poet and Peasant* by Kenneth E. Bailey, Eerdmanns 1976.

[28] Matthew 23:37.

[29] Luke 14:26.

[30] Luke 9:59-60.

plans to leave home for good?[31] Much has been written on this.[32] Unpacking the cultural details makes the following very clear; Jesus gives duty to God the highest priority, but sanctions no disrespect for parents or family.

Jesus, as a rabbi of his time, uses extreme language to convey the vast distance between love for family (good thing) and love for God (far greater thing). It is so vast that it is akin to the distance between love and hate. And yes, family duties are very important, but even so they pale when placed alongside duty to God. There will be times when tensions result in ruptures, for instance a daughter may realise that her faith conflicts with the family business' long-held tradition of defrauding the tax office. Her refusal to cook the books might result in her leaving not just the family business but also the family home. Jesus predicts that his kingdom will bring some quite devastating divisions within families[33] and that those thus forced to leave will not go unrewarded.[34]

But despite all the things that can go wrong, Jesus maintains an expectation throughout that families are a good thing and should be good.

Alongside us

Loving God,
when we are in the midst of family struggles,
keep us from being so blinkered by our pain,
that we lose sight of everyday goodness,
and become blind to fairness.
Be alongside us
as one who knows how loyalties can clash. **AMEN**

---

[31] Luke 9:61-62.
[32] See the brilliant chapter 2 'The fox, the funeral and the furrow' in *Through Peasant Eyes* by Kenneth E. Bailey (Eerdmanns, 1980).
[33] Luke 12:49-53.
[34] Matthew 19:29.

Day 5: Jesus struggled with his family when he could not fulfil his duties

When Jesus saw his mother and the disciple whom
he loved standing beside her, he said to his mother,
'Woman, here is your son.' Then he said to the disciple,
'Here is your mother.' And from that hour the disciple
took her into his own home.

John 19:26-27

The Commandment we are most likely to ignore is the one about taking one day off in seven:

I really would if it weren't for...

I certainly will review this again, just as soon as I've got through...

It's just not all that realistic in this day and age...

I'm clergy! My people need me ... here's my mobile number.

The second easiest to ignore is the fifth, the one about honouring our parents:

Well if you'd met mine...

Couldn't it be a bit more two way? Parents would be easier to honour if only they had a bit more respect for their children ...

I'm fairly sure I keep this most of the time ... certainly more than my kids do for me ...

Which one is the fifth again?

If Jesus' example is our guide then obedience to this commandment does not mean unquestioning subservience to our parents. What the Gospels tell us about the encounters between Jesus and his mother leaves much to be desired; we search in vain for something more substantial than the snippets we are granted. There's more recorded dialogue from just one conversation between Jesus and a Samaritan woman at Jacob's Well than from all his combined exchanges with his mum.

Apart from those we have already considered, there is the time when Mary tells him a wedding party is about to run dry.[35] Jesus replies to her as 'Woman' which sounds abrupt, but might be one of those cultural things where the tone has got lost over time. (All the same, I would not risk this on a visit home.) The dialogue between Mary and Jesus is scant, for such an impressive miracle. Mary tells the servants to follow his instructions and soon the party is awash with the finest wine. The story seems somehow lacking, without a final exchange between them.

Once again the huge gaps in the text push us towards the subtext. We have already looked at how obligations to parents were important to Jesus and how sharply he dealt with the Pharisees for their spiritualised attempts to dodge them.[36] Then there is one final scene where Jesus reveals the struggle of his situation. He knows that he has duties to Mary which he will not be physically present to fulfil. John's Gospel remembers Jesus giving instructions from the actual cross. As he is dying he delegates Mary's care his beloved disciple and confirms to Mary that as of now, John will now be her son.

I am familiar with the gospel writers employing a degree of licence as they structure their narratives. The way John tells this story demonstrates the strength of Jesus' love for his mother; it is too strong to be eclipsed, even by his dying agony.

I am far less comfortable with the unwritten flip side of

[35] John 2:1-12.
[36] Matthew 15:1-9.

John's account, which is that Jesus left his mother's later needs very much to the last minute. As it stands her care package is not only pitifully thin on detail but it is also hastily dictated rather than mutually agreed. This seems at odds with much we know about Jesus, not least his meticulous planning of his final days.

Perhaps we could leave it that Jesus knows the time is coming when he will not be there for his mum, so towards the end of his earthly life he makes provision for her (and hopefully they plan this together and he listens as well as instructs). Whether this is arranged from the cross or at some earlier point, his words reveal a struggle within him. His God-given mission conflicts with his filial responsibilities and he knows his mum will lose out.

He has already taught clearly about which set of duties has the ultimate priority: God first, family second. How this works out in complex everyday decisions is rarely straightforward, especially given the large overlap between obedience to God and duty to parents. In the twenty-first-century West our complexities have grown, as parents tend to live for longer and want to remain independent for as long as possible. Loneliness in old age is a now huge issue, as is the pressure on adult children to provide for the generations both above and below them. I know people nearing their own retirement who simply do not have the resources to care adequately for their elderly parents whilst raising their own children and in some cases their grandchildren too. Care for self and partners goes out the window. For worse and for better many traditional structures are disappearing. Who wants to return to the days where an extended family all live under the same roof? Did daughters-in-law and mothers-in-law ever happily share kitchen space or wisdom on child-rearing? This might work on paper but how often in reality?

We face struggles that Jesus of Nazareth never knew. He never had to have *that* conversation with Mary about how she is no longer safe to drive or for how much longer can she live on her own or about which of her valued possessions will and will not fit into her new room in sheltered accommodation. Jesus never had to hear Mary talk through her resuscitation options, fret about dementia, apologise for incontinence or grieve for yet another of her aged life-long friends.

It is good to know that Jesus sought ongoing support for his mum but is that enough to help us in our current struggles?

Alongside us

'Jesus NEVER knew what it was like to be this old!

This was barked at me by an elderly parishioner who was immediately mortified at his outburst. He had no need to apologise, but he had been raised never to snap at the clergy, no matter how dim-witted they were being, not even if he suspected they might be fumbling for some version of 'Jesus knows just how you feel'. He was right on both counts ... about what I was trying to say next and about Jesus' senior years.

How can Jesus truly be alongside us in the struggles of ageing when he died young *and* missed the dilemmas of caring for an elderly relative? The only answer we have is so very small. It might not be enough to satisfy those caught in the storm, though perhaps in time, it could spread like a pinch of yeast to fill a whole batch. We have this assurance; some of Jesus' final words reveal that he at least imagined these struggles and realised his inability to meet them alone. My hope is that their taste remains with him, even now as he is risen and ascended and that this is enough to fire his watchful imagination as he seeks to draw alongside us today.

Loving God
in all our struggles surrounding ageing
in all our juggling of competing priorities,
where decisions have to be made
without the benefits of hindsight,
where more care for one
might result in less for another,
give us wisdom
guide us to seek support,
and most of all,
give us your presence
and leaven our tiredness
with your life and love. **AMEN**

Days 6 and 7: Jesus struggled with his family... some concluding thoughts

Leo Tolstoy famously wrote, 'All happy families are alike, each unhappy family is unhappy in its own way.' [37]

There is too much we do not know, too much that was never written for us to judge whether the family home in Nazareth is, on balance a happy one or not. We have enough to tell us that Jesus' family life is far from plain sailing. And with respect to Tolstoy, I am not convinced that families can be divided so neatly into 'happy' and 'unhappy'. Families go through phases and a happy time for one member, might be riddled with dysfunction for another.

At the very least, we can conclude that God now knows what it is to be part of a human family, not from a textbook or even from careful observation but from direct personal experience. Of course, Jesus grew up in *his* family not *ours* and this was all a long time ago, so there will be very few *exact* parallels. The fact remains, however; Jesus grew up in a human family and with them he negotiated difficult days, competing agendas and conflicting expectations.

So how do we find Jesus alongside us in the heat of our family struggles? The answer is both frustratingly simple and yet, all too often in *that* moment, seemingly impossible. It is

[37] Leo Tolstoy, *Anna Karenina*.

this … we talk to him. We pray. We look for him, maybe not outwardly as looking upwards might be misunderstood as rolling our eyes and thus ramping up tension. Any prayers at this point need not be complicated, usually the shorter the better. We even could borrow directly from Peter's simple, 'Lord save me' or tweak it into, 'Jesus draw alongside us and save us'.

God understands … Jesus struggled with his family too.

Jesus struggled with his family

Questions for any time of year

1. How do you imagine Jesus' childhood?
   a. Do you think that there were 'huge volumes of everyday stability', where the gripes are 'odd lines, paragraphs and footnotes' or do you envision something else?
   b. If you were allowed to ask Jesus' family one question about his childhood, what would that be?
   c. Could you invent a missing story and write it, as if from one of the Gospels, recounting a happy family occasion?

2. Think about the younger people in your life:
   a. What kind of support do you offer them?
   b. Do you help them to grow unshackled by the past?
   c. Do you ever store up their youthful exuberances as possible ammunition for use in a future conflict?

3. Have you ever sensed Jesus alongside you when you have been with family:
   a. when things were going well?
   b. when things were going badly?

4. When it comes to family traditions:
   a. Are there any traditions that you feel you have outgrown but somehow cannot leave behind?
   b. Do you ever sense a struggle, because your family's expectations constrict you?
   c. Can you identify any occasions when your adult self reverts to a childhood role?

Jesus struggled with his family

Questions for Advent

1. How do you feel about the forthcoming 'family time' that is Christmas?
   a. Do you experience a mixture of excitement and dread and if so in what proportions?
   b. Do you live with painful memories of damage done at previous Christmases?
   c. Will you be on your own? If so, how will that be?

2. Do you recognise the phenomenon of adult children reverting to childhood roles when families come together? (If so, which role or roles do you think Jesus played in his family?)

3. Do you get much of sense of Jesus' presence in this time of family get-togethers? Is Christmas more his birthday or more a time for your family?

4. How do you feel about growing older? How confident are you that Jesus will remain alongside you in old age, despite his lack of direct personal experience?

Jesus struggled with his family

Questions for Lent

1. What advice would you give to Jesus' family as he begins his public ministry?

2. How does Jesus fit into your family?
   a. Does he unite or divide you?
   b. Can those who believe, speak openly about their convictions?
   c. Have religious opinions ever been damaging to family members?

3. Is there ever a time to step back from family? What advice would you give to someone experiencing abuse in their family home?

4. What do you think conversations were like for the rest of Jesus' family:
   a. when he disappeared for forty days into the wilderness?
   b. when he was away with the twelve, living as a wandering preacher?
   c. when it was clear he was making his way towards Jerusalem, despite all the warnings?

PART TWO

Jesus struggled with his friends

Introduction – Jesus struggled with his friends

Jesus: Beware of the yeast of the Pharisees and Sadducees.
The Twelve *(to each other)*: It is because we have brought no bread?
Jesus: You of little faith ...[38]

Jesus has a bunch of twelve male friends who often do not get him at all. They are not only friends, they are also his students. They sign up, not just for companionship but also for instruction. He is their leader, their teacher and their example and so their eyes should be open wider than if they were merely consorting with an equal. The Gospels writers make much of their failures and Jesus' remedies. This is all for our encouragement. We gain from their frequent stumbles as we too shamble along, trying to follow Jesus in our own faltering ways today.

We are stuck with our families but with our friends, we get to choose. Sometimes our friends become more like family than actual family. Armistead Maupin tells how some LGBTQ+ people, when their *bio*-logical families fail to get them, form 'logical families'; a group of close friends who become even closer than blood relatives. We do not see this exactly in Jesus but there a clear shift away from the people amongst whom he grew up. Certainly in his final years, he seems to spend the greater part of his time with his friends.

His chosen twelve friends are the cause of many headaches

[38] Paraphrase of Matthew 16:5-8.

and a great deal of frustration. In short, he struggles with them.

And just one more thing before we start, Jesus had many more disciples than this cohort of a dozen men. His wider group include women and he is financially dependent on women.[39] To help clarify this distinction, I will refer the 'the twelve' when I mean the smaller all-male group and the term 'disciple' only when I mean all his followers, women and men.

---

[39] Luke 8:1-3.

Day 1: Jesus struggled with his friends when they did not share his values

Just then his disciples came. They were astonished
that he was speaking with a woman, but no one said,
'What do you want?' or, 'Why are you speaking with her?'
John 4:27

Close friends are those rare people who instinctively 'get' us
and have 'got' us for a considerable time. We laugh at the same
jokes, we expand each other's music tastes, we travel together,
we instinctively sense each other's boundaries, we respect each
other's views, we learn from each other and we share a cluster
of common values. The times when Jesus' disciples fail to
'get' him make quite a catalogue. Sometimes it looks as if his
relationship with them is a bit too 'one way'. Can it truly be
called a friendship when he understands *them* but this is rarely
reciprocated. I suspect that all too often, he feels lonely in
their company. There are on a whole range of values they do
not share with him. Here are some...

(i) The treatment of women
When the twelve return to collect Jesus from Jacob's Well they
are astonished to find him deep in conversation with a woman,
as if this is something unlikely, undesirable or worse, immoral. In
reality it is one of the most profound conversations ever recorded.

I once spent a few chilly days on Iona. John Bell was there, and he got us all to draw up a list of all the conversations Jesus ever had. Once we had done this, he asked us to identify which of these had been held with women. If you have never done this exercise, have a go. Okay, you can guess how the page will look by the end but the process is still worthwhile. Jesus enjoys talking with women. He has intelligent, insightful and lively exchanges with women. He seems not to care about the cultural strictures of his time, which frowned on such interactions. That midday at Jacob's Well and on several other occasions his twelve disciples do not 'get' him.

I am guessing the twelve do not have too many issues with women supporting them materially and financially.[40] But they do not welcome a Canaanite woman whose daughter is suffering;[41] Judas sneers openly at a woman who generously anoints Jesus;[42] and most grievously they dismiss the women's reports of Jesus' triumph over death as 'idle tales'.[43] Mary Magdalene remains an enigma; the gospel writers hint that she has a certain status amongst the disciples but then fail to clarify what this is.

In the following centuries, the twelve's descendants all but completely forget the way Jesus spoke with women. The writer of the non-canonical Gospel of Thomas seems deeply conflicted about female inclusion and invents the following conversation which now sounds so utterly appalling,

Simon Peter said to them: 'Let Mary go away from us, for women are not worthy of life.' Jesus said: 'Look, I will draw her in so as to make her male, so that she too may become a living male spirit, similar to you.' (But I say to

[40] Luke 8:1-3.
[41] Matthew 15:21-28, Mark 7:24-30.
[42] Matthew 26:6-13, Mark 14:1-9, John 12:1-8.
[43] Luke 24:11.

you): 'Every woman who makes herself male will enter the kingdom of heaven.' *The Gospel of Thomas 114* [44]

This move, away from the praxis of Jesus of Nazareth, continued as time progressed. Tertullian (155 – 220 CE) provides a hair-raising milestone in his utterly vile treatise, 'On the Apparel of Women'. Why the Church of Jesus should value such blatant misogyny is beyond me. Google it, if you want to see how far and how quickly certain elements within Christianity forgot how Jesus engaged with women.

Many great volumes have been written on this subject and there is much more to be said but for now I will simply conclude that Jesus struggles constantly with his twelve when they do not share his values with respect for women.

(ii) Children

Some of the twelve rebuke the women who bring their children to Jesus.[45] Their actual words are not recorded but in my imagination, they mansplain like bouncers on bodyguard duty,

> 'Listen my little lovelies, Jesus is actually quite an important figure. You've seen the crowds? Good! So you'll know that Jesus is now kind of an A-lister ... i.e. very unlikely to have any interest in you and especially not in your kids. So how about taking them elsewhere? Go on my darlings! Move it! Shoo! Scoot!'

Of course I might be doing them the greatest injustice here but on the other hand I could be underestimating them; their rebuke might be even more patronising.

Jesus speaks over them, asking for the children to be

[44] Translated by Stephen J. Patterson and James M. Robinson and quoted on www.biblearcheology.org.
[45] Matthew 19:13-15, Mark 10:13-16, Luke 18:15-17.

brought to him because they are *exactly* the sort of people to whom the Kingdom of Heaven belongs. If the twelve wish to enter, they should start taking notes…

On another occasion, Jesus settles their questions about greatness in the Kingdom by placing a small child before them.[46] He then changes tack and makes dire predictions about those who hurt children.[47]

Maybe Jesus does not expect his twelve to 'get' him on this one. He knows his views are hugely counter-cultural and maybe there are unrecorded stories about how, in time, the twelve came to see children with his respect.

(iii) Violence

A Samaritan village snubs Jesus' whole group as they make their way to Jerusalem. James and John feel an appropriate response is to command fire from heaven to consume them all.[48] They earn a rebuke from Jesus, the detail of which is unrecorded but his heartbreak surely is immense. Have they learnt nothing? Were they not present at the Sermon on the Mount, or do they think that somehow all that stuff about loving enemies does not apply to them?

On the night of his arrest Jesus advises each of them to sell a cloak and buy a sword. When they proclaim they have two swords, he says 'It is enough.'[49] This seems odd coming from the man who, only a short time later tells Peter

'Put your sword back into its place; for all who take the sword will perish by the sword.[50]

Luke remembers Jesus miraculously reattaching the severed ear of one of the arresting party, which, if nothing else must offer some sort of commentary on his views on

[46] Matthew 18:1-5.
[47] Matthew 18:6.
[48] Luke 9:51-56.
[49] Luke 22:35-38.
[50] Matthew 26:52.

violence. Jesus then protests that he is not leading a violent rebellion; clubs and swords belong to his opponents.

So why does he talk about buying swords? I favour the view that recalls his frequent use of hyperbole to make a point. Here, as elsewhere the twelve do not 'get' him. When they produce two swords (as if these would be much use against armed soldiers), Jesus rolls his eyes and says, 'It is Enough!' only I hear, 'Enough, enough already!'

Even at this near crucial stage he is saying one thing and they are hearing quite another. Jesus struggles with his twelve, who despite their privileged access, repeatedly fail to share his values.

Alongside us

Jesus' twelve 'friends' are rarely 'there for him too', unlike the bright-toothed six in the US TV show. Some of these stories paint a lonely picture where Jesus is singing a song to which none of them adds a harmony or even joins in for the chorus. Instead they continue to make their own discordant racket with clashing tunes and old lyrics, retained from the time before they first sat at his feet.

We are social animals and our friendships play a vital part in our overall health. We meet people through shared experiences; some of these go on to become our friends. Usually we choose the ones with whom we share some core values. Any friendship, however, maintains the power to shock. We can uncover huge dissonances, leading us to mutter, 'Sheesh, you think you know someone and then …'

Even the most loyal friends will disappoint us at some level. The more we grow to know someone, the less we will see them through those idealised lenses, set in our early encounters. Any human, even a lifelong partner can surprise us when we discover how differently they see some key aspect of life.

Jesus makes friends with a widely diverse group of twelve men. He might not share many values with them but he is the expert at befriending. He can spy treasure hidden deeply in the least likely human souls. In one of his stories, a rich man finds something notable in his utterly corrupt steward, and commends him because if nothing else, he is shrewd.[51] Does he look in the same way at his disharmonious twelve? Does he do the same with us today? And from alongside us, can he teach us as we struggle with those who do not share all our values, even when they are our closest friends?

Loving Jesus,
did you ever feel lonely in their company?
How did you cope with being continually misunderstood,
not by opponents,
not even by servants,
but by those you called your friends?

And when I feel isolated, misquoted or snubbed,
can I trust you…
to walk alongside me?
And help me to unearth
whatever is commendable
in my faltering friends?
… and in myself?
and to quietly remind me,
that because of you,
I can never be truly alone? **AMEN**

[51] Luke 16:1-8.

Day 2: Jesus struggled with his friends when they failed to follow his instructions

'You faithless and perverse generation, how much longer must I be with you and bear with you?'
Luke 9:37-41

Ena looked genuinely puzzled. She was a delightful octogenarian whom I visited at her home, once a fortnight. There were five of us in all, Ena, three of her friends and me. We would read a bit of the Bible together and then have a chat. One week, to get the discussion started (in truth never a hard task) I asked if any of them had ever been let down by someone else. The response was instant. Their stories piled in one after the other with no breaks in between. I then asked if any of us could think of a time when we had let someone else down. There followed a profound silence. Ena looked genuinely puzzled. She shook her head, then she thought a bit more before shaking her head again. The other three were the same. We had lurched across a border, from a land overflowing with illustrative stories to a place of complete famine. All four concluded along the same lines: 'I'm sorry I really don't think I ever have ever... let down anyone ... ever ...'

If they were correct then their combined 347 years were quite remarkable. By any standard they were good, kind, reliable people but all the same, I could not believe they had never once forgotten an appointment, broken a promise, ignored an agreed instruction or failed to guard a secret.

I often thought about this exchange during my prison years where once again I met many people who, with hand on heart, could reject any notion of personal wrongdoing. Some levels of denial were astonishing. My favourite was a line that began, 'Of course on the surface it's bound to look wrong ... stabbing a police officer, but in my case I was completely ...'

... but I found I was not much interested in whatever followed. In a certain light, those who end up in prison are not so different from the rest of us, apart from the matter of scale. We all minimise our offences, maximise our grievances and impute motives to our opponents that we utterly reject from ourselves. Victimhood is simply more comfortable than a balanced perspective on our interactions, so we forget our mishaps, we grant ourselves generous allowances and we tweak history into a narrative that leaves us pretty much blameless.

Oh of course I've made the odd mistake in my time, I'm far from perfect ... I'm only human ... but that's as *nothing* compared to what they've done. And don't tell me otherwise ... they *knew* what they were doing ...'

Jesus' twelve might desire a similar airbrushing of history but the gospel writers deny them any such cover. Their mistakes are enshrined in scripture and are at times embellished by Jesus' rebukes.

I shy away from a shouty Jesus, if that is how he is on one particular day. Maybe he is not as frustrated as he sounds, maybe he says all this with a resigned smile which adds up to little more than a shrug and a: 'You guys! What are you like?'

But I find it hard not to sense some anger behind his words as he says, 'You faithless and perverse generation.'

The day in question should be a good day. It certainly starts spectacularly well. Jesus takes a mountain hike with three of the twelve and hears the commending voice of his Heavenly

Father affirming that he is indeed his Son and adding that he is loved and should be listened to. All this is witnessed not just by Peter, James and John but also by those great luminaries, Moses and Elijah. So a good day so far, that is until he finds the rest of the twelve ...

They are engaged with a father who is seeking help. He claims his son is possessed (although to us, his symptoms sound a lot like epilepsy). Either way, the remaining nine fail to help. Jesus clearly expects more from them. He blasts them before lamenting the time he still must spend with them. His Father has just said he is worth listening to and possibly he is reflecting how his twelve could take note.

It is easy to get bogged down in further questions here. Does Jesus expect his twelve to be proficient in dispensing cures for all ailments? More worrying, does he therefore expect the same from us? Do his harsh words arise purely from this rough landing among his bumbling followers, immediately after flying so high with Moses and Elijah? Is this a stand-alone incident or the culmination of a row that has been building for a few days?

Context helps. Luke tells this story shortly after a much happier one. Jesus recently gave the twelve some training and then sent them out to do his work, without him physically being alongside them. This all goes very well. We read, 'They departed and went through the villages, bringing the good news and curing diseases everywhere.' [52]

By the time this day comes, the twelve have forgotten his lessons. Jesus has expectations that they are not meeting. From this I conclude that Jesus struggles with his twelve when they let him down.

He does not give up on them. In the very next chapter he gathers a much wider group of disciples and sends them out

---

[52] Luke 9:6.

ahead of him, two by two.[53] He instructs them to heal the sick and proclaim the kingdom. They return full of excitement, saying that even demons could not stand before them. Jesus is delighted and replies,

> 'I watched Satan fall from heaven like a flash of lightning.'[54]

...which is heady stuff … so he warns them against getting drunk on this power and instead to rejoice that their names are written in heaven.

Alongside us

Do I want this frustrated Jesus alongside me when I mess up and forget his instructions? Not really … actually not at all. I have never thrived under grumpiness. I prefer Jesus when he is saying his kind, encouraging words. But maybe I need to remember this more demanding aspect of Jesus, to shake me from any delusions that he is predictable, tame or worse… that his boundless kindness renders his instructions meaningless. Maybe there is value in the shock of a botched exam. Many young motorists are mercifully less cocky after failing their first couple of driving tests. A poor but fairly explained annual appraisal might shake a complacent employee to raise their game. So leaving aside my anxieties about how he voices his comments on this particular day, I can see why Jesus has expectations of his followers. On reflection, I might cautiously welcome them.

Jesus' frustration is also helpful when I turn the tables and recall times when my own instructions have gone unheeded: the intercessor whose Sunday prayers routinely ran on for

[53] Helen Bond and Joan Taylor have a fascinating take on this phrase 'two by two'. They find a resonance with the book of Genesis and argue that these pairs of disciples, like the animals in Noah's Ark, were male *and* female. See *'Jesus' Female Disciples: The New Evidence'* broadcast on Channel 4 and ABC in September 2019.

[54] Luke 10:18.

longer than the sermon, the staff member who point blank refused to comply with a SMART target and just about anyone who promised to be somewhere and failed to turn up on time. These people make me glad that I have a risen, ascended Saviour who has personal experience of staffing issues, to teach me patience and to gently remind me, that along with Ena and her friends, I too have let others down in the past.

Teachers and parents might also breathe a sigh of relief on finding Jesus like this. He shares their feelings about all too quickly forgotten instructions. I do not have children but many of my friends do, and I have witnessed their seething attempts at self-control, on those days when their offspring casually blank everything they say. They cry,

> 'I just don't know where we went wrong with them.
> Why do they have to be such brats?'

… which is not a million miles from,

> 'You faithless and perverse generation, how much longer must I be with you and bear with you?'.

Ever living Jesus,
can you recall the taste of frustration,
when they did not listen to you?
And when we feel let down,
can you draw alongside us?
can you help us find some good words,
to express our feelings,
without scalding egos or burning bridges?
And perhaps remind us that
sometimes we too fail to listen. **AMEN**

Day 3: Jesus struggled with his friends when they were poor companions

James and John, the sons of Zebedee, came forward to him and said to him, 'Teacher, we want you to do for us whatever we ask of you.' And he said to them, 'What is it you want me to do for you?' And they said to him, 'Grant us to sit, one at your right hand and one at your left, in your glory.' *Mark 10:35-37*

Early in my curacy, I met Maria shortly after her much-loved husband Gerry died. He was only thirty-two. When I went to her home to discuss his funeral, she told me how people were crossing the road to avoid her. She understood that they were fearful of saying the wrong thing and upsetting her. This only compounded her loneliness. There was no risk of upsetting her. They could hardly make her more miserable than she was already. Gerry was dead. She missed him terribly and now that her friends were AWOL, she felt utterly alone. In hard times, companions are especially valuable.

Jesus does not choose his twelve purely so he has someone to teach; he needs and desires their company. He calls them friends not servants.[55] Surely he struggles when they fail to act like friends?

One day two of them, James and John come to him with the request, 'we want dibs on the best seats in paradise'.[56] This

---

[55] John 15:15.
[56] My paraphrase of Mark 10:35-37.

goes down like a rattlesnake in a lucky dip, at least with the other ten disciples. Their prime objection is possibly neither the brothers' vain-glorious ambition nor their presumption that such a prize is there for the asking. Maybe the ten are baulking more at the queue jumping:

> 'Why didn't I think of this first? Now I've missed my chance and thanks to them I'm doomed to spend eternity in the cheap seats.'

If this is true, the ten are little better than the two brothers.

There is something even more alarming going on here and the worst thing is that all twelve are united in utterly missing it. Jesus has just given them the most devastating news.[57] He has explained how he will soon die a nasty, painful and humiliating death. And their reaction? They squabble about the best seats in paradise. He deals patiently with James and John, asking them the questions which might help them to see how inappropriate they are being. He then addresses the whole group explaining how, for all of them, their concepts of 'greatness' need to be redefined. All the while his own news remains untouched by any further reaction. We can only guess at his loneliness.

At this point Jesus is not drowning but waving, not in a friendly manner, but rather as one seeking company for the difficult road ahead. His twelve pay as much attention to him as a stony path nurtures seed; his news is unable to take root and instead is quickly consumed in the flutter of their competing ambitions.[58]

[57] Mark 10:33-34.

[58] Matthew follows the same pattern as Mark, but in his version the request for the good seats comes not from James and John but from their mother. The tragic ignoring of Jesus' news is however the same. *Matthew 20:17-28.* Luke likewise records Jesus making three predictions of his death. The last of these is followed by the rather dismal summary; 'But [the twelve] understood nothing about all these things; in fact, what he said was hidden from them, and they did not grasp what was said.' *Luke 18:34.* He also records their argument about greatness but places it even more poignantly immediately following the Last Supper. *Luke 22:24-29.*

On three distinct occasions Jesus invites a reaction from his disciples by predicting his death. He does not expect them to change his destiny, but maybe they might alleviate the loneliness of his long walk to the cross. They choose not to. His parable of the sower[59] states that the quality of our listening is our choice. We have four basic options: no listening, shallow listening, half-listening to two things at once and finally whole-hearted, fully-focused, attentive listening. Only the last of these produces a worthwhile harvest. When Jesus is talking about something as momentous as his death, his twelve should opt for number four straightaway, but tragically they often go for the first.

There are a couple of exceptions to this. Matthew records the twelve being 'deeply distressed' following one of Jesus' predictions.[60] The other comes from Peter. He perhaps chooses the third type of listening in that he half listens to Jesus, but then reacts more to the winds and waves of his internal panic. He starts to sink and cries out to rebuke Jesus. This is not what Jesus needs and he delivers the most stinging rebuke that he gives to any of his twelve.[61] We will return to this later.[62]

Jesus struggles with his twelve when they are not the friends he needs them to be. They could be true companions, but their disinterest turns Jesus' long walk to Jerusalem into a lonely road.

This would be a much better story if, on hearing Jesus' words, the twelve all fall silent. Eventually one of them takes charge, invites everyone to sit down and then asks Jesus to say a little more. All twelve listen without interrupting and certainly without contradicting. After Jesus has spoken they take turns

---

[59] Matthew 13:1-9, Mark 4:3-9, Luke 8:4-8.

[60] Matthew 17:22-23.

[61] 'Get behind me, Satan! You are a stumbling-block to me; for you are setting your mind not on divine things but on human things.' Matthew 16:23.

[62] 5 (c) Jesus struggles with his destiny in Gethsemane.

to respond and he is assured that he has for now, their full attention and will have for the future, their companionship on the road. As they begin rising to continue their journey, only Jesus notices, that sitting silently on either side of him, are James and John.

Alongside us

Sometimes it is hard to ask for help and the more desperate the situation, the less willing we are to ask. Maybe this is because before asking we still have the hope of being heard but what of the desolation of being dismissed or of finding that there really is no help? Not asking avoids these horrors and preserves the notion that help might be out there … somewhere. Good friends notice this kind of distress. They are companions, observant and proactive in asking direct questions about needs. Jesus' twelve fail here. He asks for their help and receives very little.

Some people have a firmly fixed notion that it is wrong for them to ask for help for themselves. They fear they will appear selfish, childish, demanding, self-indulgent or even self-piteous. Jesus shows that it is okay to signal our needs for attention. He does it himself. Hopefully, we have people nearby with whom we can safely speak. If there is no one at all, there are always the Samaritans. And I cannot stress this enough: 'Care for self' is not the same as 'selfish'.

Some people might pray for help but still refrain from speaking to another human. Praying is always worthwhile. We know that, in prayer Jesus seeks God's consolation when he hears about the execution of John the Baptist [63] and when he is in Gethsemane.[64] However he also seeks conversation with friends. Sometimes praying is not enough. Sometimes we need to speak into a human ear, to see the reactions of a human face and hear answering words spoken by a human voice, even

[63] Matthew 14:13.
[64] Matthew 26:36-44, Mark 14:32-42, Luke 22:39-45.

when we know what those words will be. Pretending otherwise is aspiring to a level of super-spirituality that Jesus does not seek for himself.

We need the companionship of Jesus and of other humans when we are in crisis. We also need to draw alongside those around us. There can be a double whammy for people suffering grief or chronic pain, first there is the agony itself and then the loneliness as former friends drift away, seeking more rewarding company.

> Jesus who walked a path towards suffering,
> protect us from the same,
> but if we must walk it,
> guide us to those who can support,
> and with them,
> walk alongside us.

> Jesus who observed so carefully,
> open our eyes to see those around us,
> and our ears to hear them,
> and our mouths to risk an awkward word
> and keep us close to you,
> as we draw alongside them. **AMEN**

The vital importance of questioning and listening to those who talk about their own death.

I tried to include the following in the text above but it felt slightly crowbarred in. However when I came to remove it, I found I could not.

When Jesus talks about his own death he is not suicidal, his death defies all the usual categories. We might meet people who seem unusually low or who start saying odd, out of character things about life and death. We do well to ask clear questions and listen very carefully.

When I worked in a prison, our chaplaincy team's first daily duty was to visit everyone who had come in the previous day. We had a number of questions to raise with each of them, including whether they were at any risk of self-harm or suicide. Asking such blunt questions takes some getting used to. It is just not very British to be so direct about something so personal and catastrophic. The temptation to hedge around is almost physical but it leads to nowhere good. There are no substitutes for the words,

'Do you currently have any thoughts of self-harm or suicide?'

The answers were never predictable but could vary from, 'You're having a laugh, aren't you?' to, 'Well, never normally, but … last night … after my cell-door had been closed …'

Recently I completed the excellent online Suicide Prevention Training.[65] I strongly recommend this to everyone. It is not just for taxi drivers, taking an anxious fare to a high bridge, it is for all of us. One of the key ingredients is again risking the blunt question and using the actual word 'suicide'.

If we want to be alongside the distressed, euphemisms are not helpful. It can be very hard for those at risk to voice their feelings and to say the word 'suicide'. It is the alongsider's duty to end the silence around this and all such words. If you have never done the online Suicide Prevention Training, I urge you in the strongest terms to make time for it. It might prove valuable beyond words.

[65] www.zerosuicidealliance.com/training

Day 4: Jesus struggled when his friends abandoned him

Jesus said to them, 'You will all become deserters because
of me this night; for it is written, "I will strike the
shepherd and the sheep of the flock will be scattered."'

Matthew 26:31

There is no substitute for being there. I heard about a priest
who was a bit of local legend. He was rather shambolic and
rarely sober. He was, however, highly valued by all his parish
for the one simple fact; he always turned up. Whatever the
situation, no matter how dire, he would appear. He might not
be suitably dressed. He might not even say much. He was a
living metaphor for the local church, possibly a bit shabby and
easy to dismiss as out of date but beyond invaluable, in those
moments when someone was needed simply to be there.

Chaplaincy teams understand the importance of this.
They rightly feel alarmed by every new cost-cutting exercise.
People turn up with clipboards measuring whatever can be
measured. They ask, 'At the end of the day what does the
Chaplaincy actually do?'

At the end of the day what does the Chaplaincy actually
do? In terms of material output the answer is 'very little' and
so their feedback concludes: 'It seems all they do is talk to
people. So why are we paying good money for that?'

A prison's governing governor was once asked whether,
given a free choice, he would ditch his chaplaincy department.

His answer was telling, 'To be honest, I'm not always sure what they're up to however I am absolutely convinced that we would soon discover how much they bring if we were ever foolish enough to lose them.'

He had learnt the economically-hard-to-prove fact that there is no substitute for having people who will simply be there. The twelve might concur with him; they might even sport t-shirts and badges saying so, had such things existed back then. There is a gap however between their aspirations and their practice.

We can only guess how much Jesus struggles with them in the time we now call Holy Week. On the surface he seems resigned. In my mind he also sounds weary as he argues with Peter (but might be just my own conjecture).

> Jesus: You will all desert me, as it is written.
> Peter: I won't. Even if all the others do.
> Jesus: You will *(sighs)* … before tomorrow morning you *all* will.
> Peter: I won't. Not ever. I'd rather die.
> All the rest: Same goes for us too! [66]

The very fact that he predicts their desertion indicates an on-going struggle within Jesus. He knows his need of them and at the same time he carries the certainty that when the going gets tough, they will abandon him. Does issuing this warning afford him some small sense of control? If so Peter's well-meant but doomed protestations surely inflame rather than soothe.

For the majority, their resolutions crumble to dust the moment the arresting soldiers arrive in Gethsemane. There are some shenanigans over a cut off ear, but otherwise, they offer no real resistance before scarpering into the night.

Peter stays close enough to perform the extraordinary

[66] My paraphrase of Matthew 26:31-35.

feat of denying Jesus whilst still preening his top-disciple feathers. This all ends when a rooster awakens him to the cold light of dawn. Then along with most of the others, he is absent from the narrative until Sunday morning. John is the other exception. He appears at foot of the cross where Jesus asks him to take care of Mary. All the proactive roles are taken by the female disciples and some outsiders, Simon of Cyrene and Joseph of Arimathea. The truth is, the twelve abandon Jesus when it counts ... when he needs them most.

It is not as if Jesus has high expectations. It is hard to pinpoint exactly what he needs from them, beyond their being there. They might offer a human breach in the extreme loneliness of his trial. I often spoke with men the day after they had been in court. They all confirmed the value of family members sitting in the public gallery when they were in the dock. Their loved ones neither said nor did anything. However the simple act of being there, brought an inestimable consolation. Jesus likewise requires no intervention, no game-changing plan to transform his destiny. He is resolved to continue along the path that he believes God has set before him. All he needs is some company.

As it is, he faces first the Sanhedrin and then Pilate alone. None of the twelve, not even Peter stays alongside him once things hot up.

Alongside us

Fears around abandonment are very real. They form part of our primal make up. We are after all, the descendants of those hunter gatherers who feared being left behind or exiled from their tribe. Those who paid no heed to such fears died alone, leaving no successors to inherit their careless genes. There are exceptions but most of us need to know 'our people' are around us. Even hermits draw solace from belonging to a religious order, even if they rarely meet. At his incarnation,

Jesus entered our condition. He understands from within all our innate dreads of being deserted.

There are many ways to abandon those in need. The twelve do not fall into the following trap but many others do. We might withhold our companionship out of fear of being a nuisance. We might say, 'I would phone but I don't want to intrude ...' or, 'Well they know where I am and I'm sure they'd call if they wanted me.'

Fortunately, our modern age offers us a plethora of ways to communicate with each other, beyond phoning or visiting. A simple text, a well-chosen card or even a Facebook DM might be all that is needed to chip a crack in a friend's isolation. Those in crisis should not be burdened with the responsibility of taking all the initiatives.

Turning all this around, to those times when it dawns on us that we have let someone down, we can find new direction if we allow Jesus to draw alongside us. He has past form on dealing well with those whose boasts far exceed their delivery. We experience our own versions of Peter's discomfort when we fail to be the companion we imagined we were. We can expect Jesus to deal kindly with us whenever we are confronted by our impotence. If we can welcome him alongside us, we might even glean some tips about how we can be kinder to those whose bragging irritates us.

Sometimes the right path feels lonely. The very hardest paths might winnow out not just fair-weather friends but real ones too. Jesus somehow finds the strength to continue without his runaway friends and later to forgive them. He embodies an ancient assurance that, whatever we do and however badly we fail, God will never desert us.

'Be strong and bold; have no fear or dread of them, because it is the Lord your God who goes with you; he will not fail you or forsake you.'[67]

[67] Deuteronomy 31:6.

Jesus, can you remember how you felt
as you watched them scatter,
leaving you behind...
alone with your enemies?
Can you understand our dread of the lonely road?
What is your perspective on our conflicted state,
when friends fail us,
and we fail them?
And can you remind us when we feel least able to listen,
that you remain alongside us,
and will never abandon us? **AMEN**

Day 5: Jesus struggled with his friends when they failed to 'see' him

At the end of the film *Avatar* the credits roll upwards to the song, 'I See You'. We are first introduced to the phrase 'I see you' as a traditional Na'vi greeting which signals true recognition, the opening of more than mere eyes to take in the person before us, as they are. For the human, Jake, this 'seeing' is the beginning of a personal revolution. He arrives on the alien planet Pandora with a fixed objective - to befriend the indigenous Na'vi, win and then exploit their trust and thus gain access to their rare mineral Unobtanium. However, over the course of the film Jake falls in love with Neytiri, a Na'vi woman. He switches sides and betrays his commanders. Somehow, despite the blinkers of his mission, he manages to 'see' Neytiri in a way that shatters his previous convictions and rearranges all his former loyalties.

None of Jesus' twelve quite manages this level of 'seeing'. Each one persists with their traditional blinkers, at least until Pentecost. Most of them muddle along, unaware how out of synch they are with Jesus. Judas is the odd one out in that he takes matters firmly into his own hands. Like the others, he remains convinced that Jesus' real purpose must be to rid the land of the Romans. Why else would God send the Messiah at this time? The land is overrun with foreign troops, extorting punitive taxes to fuel a pagan regime. Surely God has heard the people's cry and answered? As Jesus approaches Jerusalem, Judas sees his inner-struggle and senses that a Rubicon-level decision is nigh.

Jesus is dithering. Sometimes the way he talks, you'd think he considering backing down and throwing it all away. What's all that ominous stuff about suffering and death, if it's not wavering at the point of victory? He needs help. He needs a shove in the right direction and maybe none too gentle a shove at that. Because once he's got started … especially if he cannot step back … there'll be no stopping him. And afterwards, when the battles are all won and the land is cleansed of all foreign armies, who will get the credit? Well Jesus obviously, but who else? Who else will be rewarded for seeing what all the others missed, for recognising that moment when Jesus needed a final push to launch him and send him hurtling in divine wrath towards the enemy? And what better push than a troop of soldiers turning up to arrest him in the middle of his prayers? It's the perfect scenario that's guaranteed to provoke the final unleashing of his full messianic powers …

Or so Judas thinks … maybe … this is again my conjecture. If however I am right, then this is where Judas is mistaken; he fails to 'see' Jesus. He has great faith in Jesus. He is undoubtedly convinced Jesus is the Messiah, otherwise what could be gained from this stunt? But he has not looked, he has not questioned *what sort* of Messiah Jesus is. This omission has devastating consequences, for both of them. Instead of being remembered as the hero of the hour, Judas has now become an enduring byword for betrayal. Dante's Inferno envisioned nine circles within hell. They are themed, in descending order: limbo, lust, gluttony, greed, wrath, heresy, violence, fraud and finally treachery. The most famous denizen of this deepest circle, imprisoned in unbreakable silent ice in a quadrant named Judecca, lies Judas. The only zone lower than Judecca is the absolute centre of hell, where the devil himself is imprisoned.

The devil has three mouths, and uses the central one to gnaw perpetually on Judas' head.

This seems rather harsh. Judas makes a tragic miscalculation but he does not set out to ruin Jesus. Far from it, he actively tries to help Jesus fulfil his destiny, as Judas understands it. Judas differs from the other eleven only in that he takes matters into his own hands. All of them fail to 'see' Jesus but only Judas takes the initiative and acts.

Even after his death, the disciples make four comments which demonstrate just how far they are from 'seeing' Jesus. The first comes on Easter Sunday morning.

(i) An 'idle tale'

When the women return from the empty tomb they tell the eleven and any others present that they have seen the risen Jesus.

> But these words seemed to them an idle tale, and they did not believe them.[68]

This term 'an idle tale' is so dismissive not just of the women but also of Jesus' own words. John's Gospel tells how Peter and the beloved disciple set off to see for themselves but the general tenor is that Jesus' closest male friends greet the first news of his resurrection by refusing to 'see' him in the reports of the first witnesses.

(ii) 'But we had hoped that he was the one to redeem Israel.'[69]

This does not come from one of the eleven but from two members of their wider group of disciples, Cleopas and another follower, probably his wife Mary. They are walking away from Jerusalem to Emmaus explaining their disappointment to a stranger. They are unable to 'see' this stranger until he

[68] Luke 24:11.
[69] Luke 24:21.

breaks bread and turns out to be Jesus himself. The gospel writers love irony and Luke surely enjoys this moment. Mary and Cleopas do not understand why their words are correct; Jesus is 'the one' and he does 'redeem Israel' but not in the Romans-removing way they are expecting. If nothing else, this incident takes some of the pressure off the remaining eleven by showing they were not alone, among the disciples in their non-seeing.

(iii) 'Unless I see … I will not believe.' [70]
Thomas refuses to believe until he sees with his physical eyes. Jesus reprimands him, telling Thomas of the blessing he has denied himself; he could have been our patron saint, the first of us to believe without seeing but instead he insisted on the old familiar way. He demands to see in the traditional way and thus fails to 'see' Jesus as Jesus now wishes to be seen.

(iv) 'Lord, is this the time when you will restore the kingdom to Israel?' [71]
The false expectations survive despite forty days of convincing resurrection appearances and presumably much discussion of all Jesus' former teaching. The disciples still do not 'see' Jesus and what he has done; they cannot shake their hope that ultimately all of this will lead to national revival.

Jesus is undoubtedly a good teacher but he clearly struggles with this class of pupils. Their basic assumptions are so rigidly fixed that not even his resurrection can dislodge them.

Alongside us

Not all friendships are supposed to last forever. There are the 'for a reason, for a season and for always' types of friends. I would prefer my friendships to end with some sort of mutual understanding that our season is over but life is rarely that simple; one side or other often believes that the relationship

[70] John 20:25.
[71] Acts 1:6b.

should last longer than the reason or the season. Some friendships are therefore hard to end. I see in Jesus a truly dogged determination not to let even one of his friends be snatched away from him.[72] He is an incredibly faithful friend who certainly does not dismiss any of his twelve even though they persistently fail to 'see' him. He never grips them so tightly that they are not free to go.[73] They can leave if they want to, but Jesus never wills this.

The truth is our lives are made richer by friends, those who breathe the same air as we do and those who do not. We risk much when we surround ourselves solely with likeminded people. The American activist Dudley Field Malone once said, 'I have never in my life learned anything from any man who agreed with me.' [74]

Birds of a feather may flock together but how much do we lose by being bird-brained? From our little Twitter bubbles the world's problems can look dangerously simple. Unlikely friendships can bless us with far wider horizons. If we can learn to 'see' people who are not like us, our lives will be so much the richer. Maybe this is yet another skill that we can learn from Jesus himself, who is the expert at 'seeing' through all sorts of differences right to the heart of whichever person is before him.

Jesus who struggled with fickle friends,
come alongside us,
open our eyes to 'see' you and
teach us the skill of building friendships,
with people who expand us,
because they are not like us. **AMEN**

[72] John 10:28.
[73] John 6:67 Jesus asked the twelve, 'Do you also wish to go away?'
[74] Dudley Field Malone, American attorney, politician and liberal activist (1882-1950). A similar quote is also attributed to the science-fiction writer Robert A. Heinlein.

Days 6 and 7: Jesus struggled with his friends ... some concluding thoughts

Following the 2016 referendum the UK became bitterly divided over Brexit. Friends are stranded on the opposing sides of Leave and Remain, each furiously convinced that their way ahead was the safest, fairest and most prosperous. Rational debate was quickly replaced by slanging matches on social media. Attempts to persuade with logic were mistrusted as people muttered about 'too many lies, from too many experts'. One of my friends (with whom I disagreed passionately about Brexit) posted the following meme,

> 'Arguing with idiots is like playing chess with a pigeon... no matter how good you are, the bird is going to shit on the board and strut around like it won anyway.'

Jesus draws alongside us, calling us his friends and loving us even when we are being stubbornly pigeon-brained. His friendships are not quite like ours. Certainly with his twelve there is the unavoidable power imbalance. He is the Son of God while they, though called friends are also very much his students. Perhaps he had other relationships that were more akin to friendship, as we know it. Mary Magdalene might be a real friend to him as might Mary and Martha too, despite the film makers' ardent desires to insert romance into every possible frame. Unfortunately, the Gospels leave us wanting so much more in their descriptions of his disciples, especially those from his wider group beyond the twelve.

So it is to the twelve that we return and finding our place within their number, we can see how he teaches us patiently that God is love, time and time again. We do not get it. We constantly underestimate love. We cling to our hurts. We maintain certain core beliefs in the face of all Jesus' evidence. We mistrust the reasoning of others. We shut down when we feel we have had too much. Against his own advice, Jesus continues to place his pearls before our muddy trotters. Why does he do this? If nothing else he is giving us an object lesson in love. Watching Jesus teach his disciples is like ticking every one of St Paul's boxes:

> Love is patient; love is kind; love is not envious or boastful or arrogant or rude. It does not insist on its own way; it is not irritable or resentful; it does not rejoice in wrongdoing, but rejoices in the truth. It bears all things, believes all things, hopes all things, endures all things. Love never ends.[75]

From his position alongside many Christians, Jesus did not reveal the win-win answer for Brexit to either side, (despite me itching to contend that he *did*, if only others had listened) but in this and in every other conflict, he can us teach us God's way of love, even love for our opponents. He can remind us that an opponent (even a politician) getting hammered on Twitter is also a human being. Clicking 'like' on a personal attack adds our weight to a gut punch and our sting to a slap on a human face.

Jesus can help us to grow in patience in the face of obdurate stupidity because he has faced so much of this

[75] 1 Corinthians 13:4-8.

already, not least from his twelve friends with whom he struggled so often. Alongside us he can teach us, again from his own experience how to grow friendships even with those who might never truly 'get' us but nevertheless, can still enrich us.

Jesus struggled with his friends

Questions for any time of year

1. Is friendship an art or something that just happens? What sort of investment and maintenance do healthy friendships require?

2. How easily do you make friendships with people who are very different from you?

3. How do we learn another person's values?
   a. Does the same apply to learning Jesus' values?
   b. How can we truly 'see' Jesus?

4. How do you respond to Jesus' statement that he calls his followers, not servants but friends?[76]
   a. What kind of friendship does Jesus offer you?
   b. How is it similar and how it is different from your other friendships?
   c. Does Jesus need your friendship? What's in it for him?

5. How would know that Jesus, in friendship, has drawn alongside you? What signs would you look for?

6. Complete the Zero Suicide Alliance online suicide prevention training[77] and discuss its contents with friends.

---

[76] John 15:15.
[77] www.zerosuicidealliance.com › training.

Jesus struggled with his friends

Questions for Advent

1. Do you find Christmas cards a joy or a chore? Are there any ways you can use them to build your friendships, rather than simply maintain them?

2. How important are friendships in the coming Kingdom?

3. Which friendships carry light into your life? Which friendships bring you joy? Are there lessons you can draw from these and apply in other friendships?

4. Can you relate to the proverb 'Well-meant are the wounds a friend inflicts, but profuse are the kisses of an enemy.'[78] Does Jesus' friendship ever work like this too?

5. Advent prepares us for Jesus' birth, the start of his ministry and his return in glory:
   a. What new ventures might Jesus be calling you towards?
   b. Will you be sent out alone or accompanied?
   c. Do you receive your calling as an individual or a member of a group?
   d. How can you and your friends best help each other to prepare for his return?

6. Complete the Zero Suicide Alliance online suicide prevention training [79] and discuss its contents with friends.

---

[78] Proverbs 27:6.

[79] www.zerosuicidealliance.com › training.

Jesus struggled with his friends

Questions for Lent

1. What role does social media play in your friendships? What effect would a fast from social media have on your friendships?

2. Have you ever been let down by a friend? Have you ever let a friend down? How do you feel about the difference between the two experiences?

3. Can you relate to Jesus feeling lonely even though he is surrounded by his friends?

4. What advice would you give to his twelve as Jesus starts his final journey toward Jerusalem?
   a. How could they, as his friends lighten his burden?
   b. How would you cope as one of his twelve, when he was clearly feeling stressed?

5. When do you find it hardest to stay close to Jesus?
   a. What pressures might make you abandon him?
   b. In the past what has been your 'quitting point'?

6. Complete the Zero Suicide Alliance online suicide prevention training[80] and discuss its contents with friends.

---

[80] www.zerosuicidealliance.com › training.

PART THREE

Jesus struggled with religious people and structures

Introduction – Jesus struggled with religious people and structures

If there were a league-table for the best insults in Shakespeare, these would be my votes for the top five:

5. 'Thou damned and luxurious mountain goat.'[81]
4. 'Get thee glass eyes, and like a scurvy politician seem to see the things thou dost.'[82]
3. 'Thou sodden-witted lord! Thou hast no more brain than I have in mine elbows.'[83]
2 'Would thou wert clean enough to spit upon.'[84]
1. 'Your brain is as dry as the remainder biscuit after voyage.'[85]

Shakespeare wrote enough of these to fill a book.[86] Jesus' insults though less fruity, were equally stinging. He did not say enough for a paperback[87] but the remarkable finding from such a collection would be that his most shocking put-downs were aimed not at Romans, drunkards, family members or off-message disciples but at religious people. Here are a few:

---

[81] *Henry V* - Act 4, Scene iv.
[82] *King Lear*, Act 4, Scene vi.
[83] *Troilus and Cressida* - Act II, Scene i.
[84] *Timon of Athens* - Act IV, Scene iii.
[85] *As You Like It* - Act 2, Scene vii.
[86] *Shakespeare's Insults. Educating Your Wit* by Wayne Hill & Cynthia J. Ottchen, Ebury Press.
[87] *The Saviour's best zingers* perhaps? Maybe not ….

'So, for the sake of your tradition, you make void the word of God. You hypocrites!' [88]

'But woe to you, scribes and Pharisees, hypocrites! For you lock people out of the kingdom of heaven. For you do not go in yourselves, and when others are going in, you stop them.' [89]

'You blind fools!' [90]

'…you are like whitewashed tombs, which on the outside look beautiful, but inside they are full of the bones of the dead and of all kinds of filth.' [91]

'You snakes, you brood of vipers! How can you escape being sentenced to hell?' [92]

And out of all of these his favourite, his most-used is simply…

'Hypocrite!' [93]

His contemporaries might wonder how the Romans manage to escape scot-free, despite their levying of taxes, to pay for the privilege of their occupation. Jesus may allude to them but he refrains from directly criticising them. The Scribes, Pharisees and Sadducees on the other hand …

In this next section, we enter into this religious crossfire to question why it happened.

---

[88] Matthew 15:6-7a.
[89] Matthew 23:13.
[90] Matthew 23:17a.
[91] Matthew 23:27.
[92] Matthew 23:33.
[93] Matthew 6:2, 6:5, 6:16, 7:5, 15:7, 22;18, 23:13, 23:15, 23:23, 23:25, 23:27, 23:29, Mark 7:6, Luke 6:42, 12:56, 13:15.

Day 1: Jesus struggled with his religious neighbours, the Pharisees

You snakes, you brood of vipers! How can you
escape being sentenced to hell?
Matthew 23:33

What would you rather have, a pebble or a brick in your walking boot? The answer is 'a brick'. Why? Because we think we can live with a pebble. We might walk with it for several miles until we finally get fed up, sit down and dig it out. We know we cannot even begin to walk with the brick. So if we find one in our boot, we remove it at once. We make no attempt to accommodate it. It never has any chance to get under the soles of our feet.

If the Romans are bricks then the Pharisees are pebbles. They are close enough to Jesus and his disciples, for the uninformed to wonder what the problem is:

'Both groups "do" God, don't they? They should get on fine. They've got loads in common!'

And maybe they have. But more often, their closeness creates discord not harmony. Each is to the other like a pebble in a boot and, because initially their differences are underestimated, their later conflicts become all the more bitter.

We are much more likely to fall out with our near neighbours than anyone else. The Gentleman Salmon explains why:

'For you must know, no enemies are so bitter against each other as those who are of the same race; and a salmon looks on a trout, as some great folks look on some little folks, as something just too much like himself to be tolerated.'[94]

The atmosphere in Manchester Prison was always interesting on the day following a local derby. Sometimes City beat United and sometimes United beat City. I discovered that it was not helpful to comment, 'But it's only football'. I also noticed no one there had strong feelings about the fortunes of Norwich City or Ipswich Town, their being too far away to present any threat, at least not to Mancunians ... to each other is a different matter.

The same dynamic is at work between Jesus and his nearest neighbours: the Sadducees, the Scribes and most of all the Pharisees. In just one outburst [95] he calls them; hypocrites, blind guides, blind fools, snakes, and a brood of vipers. He says they are 'full of greed and self-indulgence' and he likens them to 'whitewashed tombs' a grisly image of a clean exterior hiding inner putrefaction. Jesus concludes by wondering aloud how their leaders will 'escape being sentenced to hell'.

This level of outrage clearly comes from somewhere. It testifies to Jesus struggling with the Pharisees over a long period of time. They cause him far more grief than the Romans, who never truly get under his skin. The Pharisees and Jesus both promote Godly living but according to Jesus his yoke is easy and his burden light,[96] whereas he claims the Pharisees...

'tie up heavy burdens, hard to bear, and lay them on the shoulders of others; but they themselves are unwilling to lift a finger to move them.'[97]

---

[94] The Gentleman Salmon in Chapter 3 of *The Water Babies* by Charles Kingsley.
[95] Matthew 23:1-33.
[96] Matthew 11:28-30.
[97] Matthew 23:4.

Jesus maintains their teaching excludes people from God by continually increasing the number of hoops that need to be jumped through, to avoid offending God. These hoops quickly become immovable with no concessions for those with less education or resources. It seems the Pharisees did not recognise that a step for one might be a mere trifle but that same step may be for another, a hard battle.

More worrying than this, is the question about their view of God. Reading back through Jesus' critiques it seems that for them, God is a fearsome nit-picker, vindictive and easily offended by every single lapse of observance, however minor.

Jesus, in contrast claims to offer a hoop-free faith, with a door too narrow[98] for the baggage of pride and very few rules, all of which boil down to just these, love God and love your neighbour as yourself.[99]

Of course we only have Jesus' version of this conflict. It would be beyond fascinating to discover a pot of scrolls, recording their views of Jesus.

Jesus and his religious neighbours might look similar but in practice the differences between their teachings, their theologies and their expectations of their followers are immense, as is their struggle with each other.

Alongside us

In the course of our lives there will be conflicts with our neighbours over far more important matters than mere football. Perhaps love for our neighbours is even harder than love for our enemies. Often the two will overlap - and the closer they are, the more they will get under our skin. If we find fulfilling Jesus' great commandment a struggle, then we can draw strength from his own struggles. His teaching is not born simply from divine inspiration but is rooted in his own earthly difficulties. If we ever underestimate the

[98] Matthew 7:13.
[99] Matthew 22:35-40, Mark 12:28-31, Luke 10:25-28, John 13:34.

severity of these, a short trip to Matthew 23 will put us right.

No doubt the Pharisees would baulk at the suggestion that they do not lift a finger to help their followers but they can never claim to draw alongside strugglers and stragglers in the same way as Jesus. He never asks his disciples to do anything he is not prepared to do himself. He always goes first and further than they do and then comes back to support them. [100]

> Jesus can you remember the tensions,
> that led to your outbursts?
> Can you still taste your anger,
> which led you to denounce
> your neighbours' hypocrisy?
> Can you draw alongside us when we are outraged,
> understanding us,
> educating us,
> refining our protests and
> guiding us, whatever the provocation,
> to find new and old ways to love? **AMEN**

---

[100] See John 14:3 'And if I go and prepare a place for you, I will come again and take you to myself, so that where I am, there may you be also.'

Day 2: Jesus struggled with restrictive religious activity

'You hypocrites! Does not each of you on the
sabbath untie his ox or his donkey from the manger,
and lead it away to give it water?'
Matthew 13:15

My Dad used to tell me how the swings were chained up on a
Sunday. He grew up in Hastings in the 1930s in a very different
England from now. He pondered over whose job it was to
enter the park on a Saturday evening with the sole purpose
of restricting the possibility of play on the Christian Sabbath.
This all seems to belong another world, now that the Sunday
high street is indistinguishable from how it looks on any other
day.

Jesus struggles with much of the religious activity of his
day and the thinking that lies behind it. The Pharisees have
complicated rules for everything, so keen are they to avoid
even the risk of transgression. Many of their anxieties revolve
around the Sabbath. The fourth commandment begins thus:

'Remember the sabbath day, and keep it holy.'[101]

For them 'holy' means undefiled by anything that might
look like labour. Jesus accuses them of losing sight of the
Sabbath as a gift, which is very serious because when they do,
the Giver starts to look like a tyrannical regulator.

[101] Exodus 20:8.

With the Pharisees a cornfield becomes a minefield. If whilst out on a Sabbath stroll, a cloak brushes against a drooping head of corn and causes some of the grain to fall, can that be counted as harvesting and therefore work? Likewise the soles of sandals might crush the fallen grain. Is that milling and therefore once again work? Some Pharisees argue it is.

Their religious zeal is such that the gift risks becoming a trap and the day of rest, a day of trepidation on which everyone needs to stay hyper-alert to all risks of inadvertent labour. Not surprisingly Jesus confronts them. One Sabbath some Pharisees witness his disciples, not just walking through a cornfield but actually picking at some of the ears of corn.[102] Luke's account includes the detail of them rubbing the grain in between their palms adding *intentional* milling to their charge sheet.

Jesus turns the argument back to the gift (and by implication, the nature of the Giver.) He says:

'The Sabbath was made for humankind, and not humankind for the Sabbath, so the Son of Man is lord even of the Sabbath.'[103]

God is neither petty nor miserable, therefore God's gifts are neither restrictive nor misery-making. The Pharisees' many rules demand too much attention. In their world, rules become the central focus displacing God, who increasing looks like a nit-picker.

Matthew, Mark and Luke all follow this incident with the story of a man who comes to Jesus with a withered hand. Jesus heals him, gaining further opprobrium from the Pharisees since it is the Sabbath.

Luke continues this theme later when Jesus is the guest at a Pharisee's house.[104] He sees a man with dropsy and attempts

[102] Matthew 12:2-8, Mark 2:23-28, Luke 6:1-5.
[103] Mark 2:27-28.
[104] Luke 14:1-6.

to reignite the argument, only by now his opponents have learnt the sense in keeping quiet. Jesus heals the man and then asks if any of his silent critics would leave a son or even an ox at the bottom of a well, if they fell down there on the Sabbath. Their continued silence leads us to conclude that they would not. None of them wishes to admit that there are exceptions, but each would break the Sabbath if the reason were good enough. Once the edifice of the 100 per cent work-free Sabbath is shown to be cracked, what else might fracture and fall?

Jesus certainly questioned the restrictive religious activity of his day, but we do not know when he started to do this. Perhaps it was in Nazareth? Did some passing Pharisee scold him and his friends unjustly, for some playful trespass? Do Mary and Joseph face the embryonic versions of these arguments? Do they reconsider their own practice or do they hope this is Jesus' awkward teenage phase? Or did his devotional studies lead him to realise that God is not the sort of God who chains up swings once a week?' Sadly, we cannot pinpoint Jesus' awakening moments but we can imagine he struggles as he realises the power of religious people to restrict life.

Alongside us

The older Mr Emerson watches with dismay as the Reverend Eager stops the carriage. They are in the hills above Florence, dressed in their Edwardian finery on a beautiful summer's day. The clergyman has just noticed, that contrary to earlier assurances, the driver's companion is not his sister but clearly his girlfriend. The man of God insists that she climbs down before they drive any further. She is then left alone to walk back to Florence unaccompanied, while the English party continues on its merry way to Fiesole. Mr Emerson protests,

'Do we find happiness so often that we should turn it off the box when it happens to sit there?'[105]

[105] E.M. Forster, *A Room with a View* (1908).

Sadly, the answer seems to be yes, we do. The Church has an astonishing record of squashing happiness. How many loving relationships have been dismissed as immoral? How many times has a joyful noise been silenced by the tired and irritable? How many of God's gifts have been dismissed, because they were given to a non-European, a woman, a differently-abled person, a child or to the wrong sort of man? We have made the narrow way into a dull way and our needle's eye, while welcoming the wealthy has denied a passage to the exuberant. My fellow trainee-vicar, now the Reverend Margaret Johnson, had a wonderful knack of cutting to the chase. She would categorise college activities, students and staff as either 'life-affirming' or 'life-denying'. In her view, Mr Emerson would be on Jesus' life-affirming side, whereas the Reverend Eager, despite his supreme confidence, is in for a shock.

It is generally agreed that the older we get, the more conservative we are likely to become. We need Jesus alongside us to cajole us away from false nostalgia, judgmental suspicions about young people and self-righteous assumptions that these days, other people are bound to do everything wrong.

Most of all we need Jesus' help to continually turn us back to God. It is all too easy to get fixated by rules and thus drift away from the Rule Maker, whose first and all-encompassing rule, is love. Sometimes denominations with the harshest rules seem to do best, at least in terms of numbers; in fast changing world, their concrete certainties appeal.

Unusual restrictions are also attractive as they offer adherents that sense of being set apart from the common herd. Latter Day Saints are distinctive for their caffeine ban, the Amish for their avoidance of buttons, the Witnesses for their aversion to blood transfusions, the Roman Catholics for their insistence on a celibate male priesthood and the Anglicans... well, we are a broad church but all the same we create internal distinctions such as high or low, inclusive or conservative.

The truly devout get to wear costumes, such as wimples, dog-collars, copes and mitres. Jesus asks us to be distinctive not by our clothing nor by our unflinching, uncompromising adherence to any list of rules, but by our love.

> 'I give you a new commandment, that you love one another. Just as I have loved you, you also should love one another. By this everyone will know that you are my disciples, if you have love for one another.'[106]

This is much harder to perfect, so we revert to defining our identities by our outfits and ordinances.

The flip side of questioning Sabbath observance is that now, 2000 years later on, we proceed as if we have no need for a day of rest. The pendulum has swung so far in the opposite direction that we need to help to reset the balance. Even when we rationalise the commandment to 'one day off in seven' we still paid little heed to it. Clergy can be the worst offenders at treating this as a nice-suggestion-if-I-can-manage-it. We know that it is always okay to pull our wayward oxen out of wells, but is there not one day a week that we could keep free from shopping or catching up on emails? Ignoring a gift altogether is perhaps even more abusive than over-policing its use.

God does not desire to restrict us or make us bored, but maybe once a week, if we take our faces away from our screens, we could learn to enjoy the company of those *physically* present.

Perhaps Jesus can draw alongside us as one who understood the Sabbath as a gift and gift to be welcomed and enjoyed? Maybe other Jewish friends who still take the Sabbath seriously could educate us a bit here?

[106] John 13:34-35.

Jesus draw alongside us,
cajole us
broaden us
relax us
knead us
stretch us
train us and
trail us
away from our safe limits
and ever Godwards
to love and love and love. **AMEN**

Day 3: Jesus struggled with excessive religious activity

'And whenever you pray, do not be like the hypocrites; for they love to stand and pray in the synagogues and at the street corners, so that they may be seen by others.'

Matthew 6:5

I have a terrible confession to make. A few years ago, I was sitting all robed-up in a cathedral, struggling to stay awake as we moved into the *second* hour of an ordination service. The droning set-prayers were interminable. I raised my head and forced my eyelids open, all too aware of the jibes I would later receive, should l lose it and start snoring. My gaze wandered around seeking a focal point. I caught a gleam of silver and followed it to a cluster of large mismatched goblets on a richly clothed table. My next thought is the one I am not proud of but suddenly there it was, right at the front of my mind.

'Oh ****! Not communion as well!'

Something has gone deeply wrong somewhere here. I will take some of the blame; there are some very obvious flaws with my patience, my attention span and my devotion. I chastened myself by recalling Jesus' words to his dozing disciples in Gethsemane ... but even then I wanted to whine to God, 'But I *have* watched with you *and* for well OVER one hour ... which, for the record wasn't exactly brief.'

A portion of responsibility must however lie beyond me, maybe in the cathedral or in the liturgists or in the very establishment of the Church of England. Why does something so joyful in essence, need to be stultifying in delivery? I also wondered how the ordinands' relatives were bearing up, especially those not used to church. This over-extended religious marathon is hardly a welcoming introduction to the joy of knowing Jesus.

I have never been good with over-long events, least of all church services. Boredom and God do not mix well in any scenario, least of all in worship. I will own part of the problem but not all of it. Some religious activity is excessive and kills joy. There is more than a whiff of blasphemy whenever devotion to the living God is made so tedious.

On a much more chilling note, there are far too many stories of religious devotion providing a cloak for murderous intent. On 22 May 2017 a young man killed twenty-two people and also himself, at the end of an Ariana Grande concert in Manchester. He might have deluded himself that he was doing this for God. He was not. His actions have nothing to do with God or with Islam, his chosen religion. If any of his motives began in devotion, they had long since departed. Such senseless cruelty is anathema to Islam. The media often colludes with such terrorists by calling them 'Islamists'. They are not, no more than members of the Ku Klux Klan are Christians. For us here in this chapter, these people serve only to prove the extreme dangers of excessive religious activity.

The problems are born when the prime focus moves away from God to what we might be expected to do for God. Jesus sees the symptoms in his religious rivals. Mercifully, their focus has nothing to do with the destruction of others and is much more about their own self-aggrandisement. He criticises those who make a big show about their praying, ostentatiously making pious noises on street corners. They get noticed and maybe someone is impressed. 'Look at him praying. Isn't he holy? I wish I could be like him.'

They receive their reward in full here on earth.

The same applies for fasting[107] while wearing a big badge, 'Look at me I'm fasting!' and for giving alms, if accompanied by a trumpet fanfare.[108]

According to Jesus, true devotion goes hand in hand with trust. Religious activity should be all about God. We have no need to attract further attention for ourselves, if we trust we already have God's full attention. The same goes for our giving. We should give without making a big show. We miss the point whenever our prime motive is impressing others.

When I lived in London I made friends with an older woman who had lost her sight. She sometimes spoke out of turn, always with the defence she was not as aware of her surroundings as the rest of us. I suspect, even hope that occasionally this was not the case. There was the evening when we were all assembled for an ecumenical meeting. We were listening to a frustrated Yorkshireman berating us for our inconsistency in prayer. He knew he was right; we were not praying hard enough and this was clearly evidenced by our empty pews: 'The problem is you don't know the power of prayer. Me? I pray! I pray every day! I pray every day for five hours a day!'

The impressed silence following this was punctured by my friend's loud cockney whisper, 'Yeah and I'm a bleedin' liar an' all!'

I was never convinced by her later protests, that she only ever intended this as a quiet aside for her neighbours. Everyone there heard it. To the speaker this was probably akin to a fart in an elevator but to me it came as a home-time bell, releasing me from an unattainable level of duty-dominated devotion.

Alongside us

Being a committed Christian can involve a great deal of activity: church services, prayer meetings, synods, young

107 Matthew 6:16-18.
108 Matthew 6:2-4.

peoples' programs, food banks, choirs, Alpha/Start courses, prison visiting, mission trips, soup kitchens, fundraising, prayer walks, committees, committees and committees. Some of this activity will be good and godly. Some will start well but then descend into some ghastly religious *Groundhog Day* trap. Some will be other people's activity but we have leapt in or held on to it, feeding our own delusions that we are indispensable. Some will be the enforced requirements of a denomination. Some will be tradition for the sake of tradition. Activism, even that which starts well, can become like a drug that repeats the lie, if you are very, very busy you are very, very important and you must be doing the right thing.

The first hymn I truly loved, ends thus:

> *Love so amazing so divine*
> *demands my soul, my life, my all.*[109]

It has taken me a ridiculously long time to realise that 'my all' includes my common sense, my commitment to rest, my need to look after myself and my duty to use my mind wisely. It is not all about exceeding expectations. God gives us the Sabbath and we should not discard it en route to any altar labelled 'achievements'. 'Love so amazing' should not launch us into frantic unthinking activity, any more than it should tie us to controlling or time-served traditions.

How often do we accept our current practice as inviolable? Do take time to ponder what kind of God lies behind some of our activities? Just as an example, why do so many religious festivals require so many dead animals? Turkeys at Christmas, lambs at Easter and fish from our depleted oceans each Friday; is this God's desire? And if Jesus draws alongside us, what might he say about welfare, cruelty, greed and sustainability. More to the point we might find him ahead of us, waiting for us to catch up and voice our protests.

[109] 'When I Survey The Wondrous Cross', Isaac Watts (1707).

Jesus keep us questioning,
keep us ever looking behind our programmes,
events, busy-ness and policing,

and as one who always kept your focus on God,
draw alongside us,
share that same focus with us and
alert us as we begin to drift away
away from God and into religious excesses. **AMEN**

Day 4: Jesus struggled with the religious establishment

A couple of times a year my friend Simon used to bring small groups of trainee vicars to spend a day with me in prison. I would do my best to explain the role of chaplaincy in the hope of sowing seeds that might one day result in new recruits for the service. Simon had an annoying habit of asking me, on each visit, a question which I found uncomfortable, like 'Henry, how do you exercise a prophetic ministry in this place?'

This touched a bundle of raw nerves made of the awkward questions that I struggled with. Why was I there and for whom? Was I there for the prisoners? For the wing staff? For the management team (at whose table I also sat) or for myself and my mortgage repayments. I believe I joined with the hope of making a difference in the lives of prisoners, however I soon discovered how hard it was to be truly incarnational among them. I ministered from a position of extreme privilege. I carried the keys that opened and locked their cell doors. I had far greater access to information. I saw my family whenever I chose. I went home each night and spent several weeks a year aboard on holiday. While I holidayed around the world, they shuffled back and forth between their wings and workshops; their longest trips being either to court or to another prison. I had found it hard enough to stand alongside people in my parish, since no one else in my part of Salford lived in a seven-bedroomed mansion. In prison this was even more difficult. More than ever I felt the risk of becoming a mere functionary in an establishment.

Sometimes I mused that the most effective prison-priest would be also a prisoner. He would be truly alongside the other men in ways I could never be. This was not an option I wished to pursue so I lived with the awkwardness. The discomfort was partially allayed by my responsibilities towards the staff as it was much easier to draw alongside them without the barriers of privilege. All the same Simon's persistent question reminded me of the queasy dis-ease of my position.

I am not alone in this. George Zabelka's case is far more extreme. He was the American Air Force chaplain who gave God's blessing to the planes before they flew to Hiroshima and Nagasaki, carrying the atomic bombs. He grew to be so haunted by his actions that he made a penitential pilgrimage to Japan on the fortieth anniversary of the bombings. Over time he had grown convinced of a terrible mismatch in his allegiances to God and to his employer.

Religious people seem doomed to participate in an uneasy struggle with the wider world and especially with the Establishment (with a capital 'E'; that informal network of self-preserving elites drawn from the aristocratic, judicial, military, economic, ecclesiastical and political spheres in any human society). We cannot ignore the Establishment, we have to engage with it, but there will always be awkward moments. These boundaries are very deeply confused within the Church of England since it is so thoroughly enmeshed in the Establishment.

Shakespeare's Archbishop of Canterbury goads Henry V to war with France. He exhibits no struggle between his desire for England's and Jesus' beatitude about peacemakers; the former eclipses the latter. Henry has qualms about the woes of spilling innocent blood but his most senior spiritual advisor dismisses these:

'Gracious lord,
Stand for your own; unwind your bloody flag'

He evokes memories of the king's noble forebears foraging in the blood of French nobility before promising to pour out the church's wealth for this fresh campaign:

'In aid whereof we of the spiritualty
Will raise your highness such a mighty sum
As never did the clergy at one time
Bring in to any of your ancestors.'[110]

We hope that Shakespeare is indulging in caricature here. We expect those 'of the spirituality' to struggle more when faced with awkward questions. Today's world requires us to ask:

- Why do Church of England Bishops, elected by no one, get to sit in Parliament?
- Should Westminster Abbey host a thanksgiving service to celebrate fifty years of the nuclear deterrent?
- Why should an atheist Prime Minister have any say in the appointment of senior clerics?
- What happens when the secular state legalises same-sex marriage but the powerful in the established church refuse to comply.
- Should the Church be subject to the same employment, equality and safeguarding laws as everyone else?

Many of our current bishops can be frustratingly absent from the public debate, preferring their 'collegiate silence'. This delays their pronouncements until they have all reached an internal consensus (and on certain subjects they never manage this).

[110] *Henry V*, Act I, scene 2.

It seems the closer a denomination buddies up to the Establishment, the more perks it accrues and the harder it becomes to exercise any prophetic ministry. When the state is going badly wrong the church has a clear duty to speak truth to power. Should Britain's churches remain neutral over issues such as Brexit, foreign interference in elections, cuts to welfare provision, the handling of the pandemic, the treatment of the Windrush generation, the implementation of Universal Credit and tax breaks for the wealthy or should the Church speak loudly to ensure the wellbeing of the most vulnerable in our society?

Jesus is clearly uneasy with the religious establishment in Jerusalem. He could never be called its chaplain or its protector. He denounces the Scribes who enjoy its trappings: the instantly recognisable outfits, the salutations in the street and the invitations to the best seats.[111] He criticises them when they pray over-loud and over-long prayers in public purely to boost their reputations as hyper-pious; they, like those who make a song and dance about giving and private fasting, have already received their reward in full.[112]

The perks and pitfalls of being publicly religious are very much alive; one of my friends always wears his dog collar on flights and often gets upgraded free of charge. Another friend (this one an atheist) treated herself to a first-class train journey and found herself sitting opposite a bishop. He was looking resplendent in his purple. She hoped his collar might be a sign that he was 'on-duty' but he ignored her smiles and returned his attention to his sheaf of very important documents. She later mused: 'I assumed that since he was wearing the uniform, he would be up for a chat.'

Anyone who has been in religious circles for any length of time will have seen someone like the Scribes, who relishes their loud, important praying voice, but leaves the rest of

---

[111] Matthew 23:5-7
[112] Matthew 6:5

wondering to whom they are speaking. Those us of used to doing the upfront stuff might even catch ourselves in this act.

People tend to respect the religious members of the Establishment, so we need to proceed with heightened awareness. Collusion is seductive; we can play along, enjoying the prestige without asking how often we are providing a smiling face for a wider system, which is possibly engaged in some ungodly purposes.

Simple avoidance of the wider world, including the Establishment is not permitted. Jesus expects his followers to be as salt and light in the world and as visible as a city on hill.[113] Later he prays they will struggle well, with the paradox of being *in* the world but not *of* the world: 'I am not asking you to take them out of the world, but I ask you to protect them from evil.'[114]

We have a tightrope to walk, a balancing-act to perform, making our way between the Scylla of over-compliance and the Charybdis of purist isolation. If we are too standoffish, we will never function fruitfully. If we are too cosy, we risk becoming the state's poodle or its dispenser of opiates. We constantly need to address these awkward issues, which might have no easy answers. If we are lucky we have friends like Simon, who will draw alongside us and keep us questioning.

There are limits to Jesus' criticism of the Jerusalem Establishment. When he rebukes his over-competitive disciples, he invites them to picture certain Gentile rulers lording their authority over their subjects. Then he lays down his own rule, 'It will not be so among you; but whoever wishes to be great among you must be your servant.'[115]

He could continue with his usual struggle, citing the poor practice of Scribes, Pharisees and Sadducees. However, when he needs a paradigm of abusive authority, he chooses to look

---

[113] Matthew 5:13.
[114] John 17:15.
[115] Matthew 20:26.

overseas to the tyrants of the great Gentile empires. He does not mention Caesar by name but it is surely not too great a stretch to imagine his gaze is heading towards Rome.

Alongside us

It is good to know that Jesus struggled with the dilemmas of living both faithfully with God and fruitfully within the wider world. Walking alongside us, he is our invaluable guide.

He can also be our strength when we need to challenge redundant privileges. We will face the rebuttal:

'It's always been like this, so accept it. Don't rock the boat. Don't take a sledgehammer to an admittedly imperfect system that mostly works.'

Behind this kind of dismissal, lurk all manner of unpleasant things, from everyday vanity, to abusive control and at the farthest extremes, sexual exploitation, terrorism and murder. Things get hushed up to maintain appearances. My home ground is the Church of England whose establishment has a shameful history of marginalising survivors of clerical abuse. Those who speak up about their hurts, have all too often been treated as the problem, while their abusers have been afforded a measure of protection.[116] This might protect the Church's reputation, for a while but I cannot imagine how bad it looks in God's eyes.

At some point, Jesus decides to ask awkward questions. He understands these will be unwelcome and will make trouble for him. As we struggle to frame our own difficult questions, we can ask him to draw alongside us to encourage us and give us the benefits of his experience.

---

[116] See *To Heal And Not To Hurt: A Fresh Approach to Safeguarding in Church* by Alan Wilson and Rosie Harper (Darton, Longman and Todd, 2019) and *Letters to a Broken Church*, edited by Janet Fife and Gilo, Ekklesia 2019.

Jesus, how often did you struggle to find your balance,
when dealing with the Establishment?
Please walk alongside us,
guiding us through a very different world.

Jesus, do you remember your anger
at those who loved their reputations too much?
Please awaken this anger in us.
Plant in us,
the determination
always to see-the-human
and an insatiable desire
for your kind of justice. **AMEN**

Day 5: Jesus struggled with the Temple

'Destroy this temple, and in three days I will raise it up.'
John 2:19

We might at first glance, think that Jesus is simply opposed to the Jerusalem Temple. He talks about its destruction without hyperbole, calmly making his devastating prediction as if were an already established fact.

> 'Truly I tell you, not one stone will be left here upon another; all will be thrown down.'[117]

Even more worrying is his threat to destroy the Temple himself and rebuild it in just three days.[118] This, more than anything else, gives his enemies a convenient hook on which to hang all their other objections.[119]

Our contemporary alarms go into overdrive when religious figures start talking about mass destruction. In the first half of 2019, we witnessed attacks on mosques, synagogues and churches, in New Zealand, the United States and Sri Lanka. Jesus is not planning any such outrage. His relationship with the Temple is far more complicated than simply desiring its ending.

---

[117] Matthew 24:2, see also Mark 13:2, Luke 21:5-7.
[118] John 2:19-20.
[119] Matthew 26:61, 27:40 Mark 14:58, Mark 15:29.

We hear him speaking out, both in favour of the Temple and against it. As a twelve-year old he calls it 'my Father's house'.[120] Towards the very end of his earthly ministry (or at the very start according to John) he uses the same phrase, 'my Father's house' as he overturns the tables and drives out the livestock: 'Take these things out of here! Stop making my Father's house a market place.' [121]

So he cannot be anti-Temple per se, but he is extremely critical of the way it uses its power.

He is also critical of many who attend the Temple, those who give lavishly but not generously[122] and those who pray ostentatiously.[123] He faces down the chief priests and elders of the people, informing them that, in the journey to righteousness, they are lagging behind tax-collectors and prostitutes.[124]

Imagine you are one of the chief priests and with a friend decide to listen to Jesus. You are both curious about him. You have heard many conflicting stories, but you want to suspend judgment until you have heard him for yourselves. Jesus addresses the crowd of which you are a part and tells a story about a man who owns a plot of land. This man decides to plant a vineyard. He fences it off, digs a wine press and builds a watch tower.

You might turn and catch your friend's eye. You both shrug wondering what the fuss is about. So far so ordinary … in fact this sounds just like a story Isaiah once told.[125]

Jesus then explains how the landowner plans to travel and so he leases his vineyard to some tenant farmers.

Your friend whispers, 'He's telling it wrong. He plants a vineyard and the vineyard produces sour grapes and so he knocks it down. That's how the story should go.'

[120] Luke 2:48-49.

[121] John 2:16.

[122] The story of the Widow's offering, Mark 12:41-44, Luke 21:1-4.

[123] The parable of the Pharisee and the Tax-collector, Luke 18:9-14.

[124] Matthew 21:31b-32 (following the parable of the two sons).

[125] Isaiah 5:1-7.

Jesus continues, saying how the problems start at harvest time, when the rent is due.

You think, 'Okay this really is a departure from Isaiah, but as the owner and the founder of the vineyard, the landlord is entitled to a share of the profits. That's how tenancy agreements work.'

But Jesus tells how the tenants refuse to make their payment. The slaves sent by the landowner get beaten up, killed and stoned. This happened several times.

You and your friend again exchange glances. You guess where this is going. Jesus started with Isaiah but he has now moved on to all the prophets, who were often met with real hostility. You already know their sad stories. You also know where their tombs are and possibly you are in the habit of visiting them to say prayers.

Then Jesus introduces a new character. The landowner is certain that his wayward tenants, no matter how badly they have behaved thus far will respect his son. So he sends him.

At this point your friend nudges you and whispers, 'Who do you think he means by that? There's nothing like this in Isaiah.' You shush him and carry on listening because you are not sure either. Jesus describes the tenants' plot to kill the son and thus secure their hold on the vineyard.

'That's ridiculous. They'll never get away with it,' your friend says and none too quietly. And they do not. After they have killed the son, the owner returns, retakes control of his vineyard and exacts an awful punishment on the tenants before appointing new people to their posts. Jesus ends by quoting those verses from the psalms about the stone that was rejected becoming the cornerstone.

By now you are deeply puzzled as to what he will say next. He looks out at all the gathered chief priest and elders of the people and says:

'Therefore I tell you, the kingdom of God will be taken away from you and given to a people that produces the fruits of the kingdom.'

And you sense that when he says 'you' he means *you*. You mutter to your friend, 'Did I hear that right? He saying that *we*, that is us today … *we* are the same as those who mistreated God's prophets in the past? How can he when we do so much to revere the prophets of old? And what was that about our 'tenancy' being over? This is dangerous … he shouldn't be saying any of this … someone needs to stop him … but look at the crowds, they're loving him so now's not the time.'

You and your friend leave, certainly feeling 'got at', but also unable to shake a feeling which is less like '*something* is changing' and more like '*someone* has arrived'.

Earlier on Matthew remembers Jesus making this very same point but without the accompanying parable.

'I tell you, something greater than the temple is here.'[126]

His opponents should have been far more alarmed by the parable of the wicked tenants than any of Jesus' other pronouncements about the Temple. He says none of this lightly. He knows he is stepping into a minefield and he struggles to frame, as carefully as possible, his criticisms of the failing institution that he also regards as his Father's house.

Alongside us

Jesus recognises what is temporary and what is eternal, what can be held lightly and what must be clung to. Only with him the second 'what' is always a 'Who'. He is not spooked by the collapse of great institutions or even the movement of mountains. Alongside us he can free us the fears which insist on preservation at all costs and which ultimately take our attention away from God.

We live in a world where the mighty and unshakeable can

[126] Matthew 12:6.

disappear almost overnight. Twenty years ago a British person wandering down a high street could step into a Woolworth's to buy film from Kodak or Polaroid (just around the corner from the music cassettes). Who could have predicted all these demises? The High Street, as an institution is not guaranteed to last; it might just starve to death as we increasingly feed only the online retail giants. Their time might be now but who can say how long they will last?

No physical building is immune from the march of time. Atrocity and accident can speed things up. We watched in horror as the flames engulfed the roof of Notre Dame and its steeple fell, but all buildings will eventually return to dust. One day even New York will join Siam Reap, Merv, Memphis and Pompeii in the list of once-flourishing but now deserted cities.

In fact New York's time might come sooner than we expect, given the worrying changes wrought by the climate emergency. Currently these affect the developing world more than the West, but rising sea levels could soon threaten the rich coastal cities.

We live with the myths of continuity, despite all the evidence around us. It is unsettling to dwell for too long on our transitory existence. Faith can bring a great deal of reassurance. Perhaps God has hard-wired us to long for permanence. The trick is never to seek it in institutions, traditions or bricks and mortar. God alone is our unchanging security.

Jesus draw alongside us
and show us how to loosen our attachment,
to things which won't last.
Open our eyes to see,
One greater than the Temple.
Teach us your faith,
so that we will always seek
our eternal security
alongside you. **AMEN**

Days 6 and 7: Some further thoughts about the tragic distortion and amplification of Jesus' struggles with religious people

One of the most, if not *the* most shameful aspect of Christianity is its history of ungodly animosity towards Jewish people, ranging from casual disrespect to actual genocide, and every ghastly thing in between. Hatred is always irrational and wilfully ignores key facts. When the Church and wider 'Christian' culture persecute Jews, they perversely look to the Gospels for justification. Their favourite verses are those associated with Jesus' struggles with religious people and structures. For instance, a group representing the religious establishment shout back to Pilate,

'His blood be on us and on our children!'[127]

Matthew states this comes from 'the crowd'. Those needing little encouragement to hate Jewish people seem to imagine that all Jerusalem speaks at that moment with one voice, when in reality the 'crowd' is a group only large enough to fill the court room before Pilate's judgment seat.

Anti-Semitism is so very wrong on far too many levels to be dealt with adequately here. I will restrict myself to four pointers, which signpost the sheer corrupt, cruel, ungodly idiocy of using the Gospels to justify it.

[127] Matthew 27:25.

(i) forgetting that Jesus was Jewish

A picture has been fashioned of a noble blond teacher, from somewhere in northern Europe, having his God-given aspirations disrupted by 'the Jews' who in devilish spite, conspire to have him murdered. Following this twisted 'logic' the case is quickly settled that all Jews for ever after, are 'Christ killers' and therefore deserving of whatever wrath comes their way.

Is Jesus critical of some Jewish people and certain aspects of Jewish society? Yes. Did he struggle with some contemporary religious activities practices and the religious establishment? Yes. Does that make him anti-Semitic? Well, only if my friend Marie has to be deemed 'anti-Anglican'. On paper, online and in person she can make some extremely stark comments about the Church of England. Suppose in future generations some anti-Anglican group were to discover her tweets, they might start quoting her and using her face on their posters. They would have to ignore all the evidence of her deep commitment to Anglicanism, to the point of training for ordination as a priest. If Marie could see this future, she would be appalled, not by what she had once said but at how brutally she was being misquoted. She also has some choice opinions about Mr Johnson's conduct as prime minister. These likewise cannot be used in the future, as proof that she is anti-British. We can only imagine what Jesus makes of the unconscionable hate crimes against Jewish people and Judaism, committed supposedly under 'his banner'.

(ii) Translation issues

A quirk of New Testament Greek is to describe a crowd of individuals with a collective noun, based on the ethnicity of the majority. So any group which is predominantly Jewish will appear as 'the Jews' or '*oi Ioudaioi*'. Following this practice, a group of Irish women travelling to Brussels to protest against the climate emergency would be called, 'The Irish.' And a gospel writer might then produce the following line,

'All the Irish demonstrated loudly in the city square.'

It would be a ridiculous stretch to then imagine that this one group somehow represented all Irish people everywhere for all time. We must apply the same principle as we read verses such as:

Therefore the Jews started persecuting Jesus, because he was doing such things on the sabbath.[128]

The Jews answered him, 'Are we not right in saying that you are a Samaritan and have a demon?'[129]

The Jews took up stones again to stone him.[130]

An accurate translation would capture the fact that these were small groups of men, most of whom *were* Jewish and also members of the then religious establishment. As these verses stand they could falsely imply that all the Jews at that time, were united in persecuting, demonising and stoning Jesus. This is manifestly untrue. Modern day versions of the Bible continue to get this wrong, perpetuating an appalling stigma against modern day Jewish people and Jewish beliefs.

(iii) The Gospels clearly cite Jewish people supporting Jesus
All those called disciples in the four Gospels are Jewish. Jesus' parents are Jewish. Jesus' supporters and benefactors are Jewish. The 'daughters of Jerusalem' who wept for him are Jewish; this is a term for the poor encompassing both males and female.[131] Arimathea is in Judea so presumably Joseph of Arimathea is also Jewish, so Jesus is buried by a Jewish man. Ignoring these facts while fabricating the charge

[128] John 5:16.
[129] John 8:48.
[130] John 10:31.
[131] Luke 23:28.

of murder against all Jewish people, lies somewhere far beyond stupidity.

(iv) Several Pharisees supported Jesus

Most of the stories involving Pharisees run on the same basic tracks; Jesus does or says something spectacular, then along come the religious experts, nit-picking, complaining and trying to trip him up. However there are significant exceptions to this:

- The Pharisee, Nicodemus is so intrigued by Jesus that he visits him at night to question him. Later we see him speaking out for Jesus within his own group of Pharisees[132] and finally providing a generous gift of spices for Jesus' burial.[133]

- Jesus is sometimes a guest at the homes of different Pharisees. Admittedly these events are not the most cordial but neither are they murderous. Jesus and his opponents were able to disagree *and* share meals together.[134]

- A group of Pharisees are so concerned for Jesus' welfare, that they go out of their way to warn him of Herod's murderous plans.[135] It is hard to imagine these same people as members of 'the crowd' bellowing at Pilate, 'Barabbas' and 'Crucify him' or even joining their colleagues to insist that Pilate place a guard on the tomb.[136]

Clearly not even the Pharisees are all the same.

The people of Jesus have no business distorting the Gospels to fuel ungodly hatred. The previous chapter has been all about Jesus arguing with his religious neighbours and

---

[132] John 7:45-52.
[133] John 19:39.
[134] Luke 7:36-50, 14:1-14.
[135] Luke 13:31.
[136] Matthew 27:62-63.

criticising the religious establishment. We need to be very clear that Jesus' struggles then, can never justify any form of anti-Semitism.

In today's world, I see a clear distinction between anti-Semitism and holding accountable any government, including Israel's, for their human rights record. I deplore the brutal injustices that so many Palestinians currently experience.

However I recognise no reading of the Bible and no supposed allegiance to Jesus that can ever legitimise any abuse of Jewish people. If we ever imagine Jesus is alongside us, in any anti-Semitic act, we are dangerously deluded.

Jesus struggled with religious people and structures

Questions for any time of year

1. Which church activities awaken you to the presence of Jesus?

2. Are there any church activities that dampen rather than enliven your faith?

3. How do today's religious establishments bring joy and how do they kill joy? *Try to focus on the one you adhere to most, rather than criticising those of others'.*

4. Do you ever encounter Jesus in settings that have nothing to do with church?

5. What would you do if you felt that your religious establishment or denomination was acting counter to God's intentions (as you understand them)?
    a. When is the right time for disobedience?
    b. And how should this be expressed?

6. If anyone were to discover a pot of scrolls recording the Pharisees' views of Jesus, what might they say? *Let your imagination take you on a journey!*

Jesus struggled with religious people and structures

Questions for Advent

1. Churches can ask a lot of us during Advent.
    a. Which services and activities do you most look forward to?
    b. Which leave you exhausted?
    c. Are there any that you dread?

2. What kind of God lies behind your activities? If all your religious activities in Advent could be gift wrapped and offered to Jesus of Nazareth on his birthday, would he find gifts appropriate for his values and character?

3. Will you take any days off to rest during Advent?

4. Our global politics seem full of 'wars and rumours of wars'. Intolerance seems more acceptable than it was a decade ago. What can you do from your small corner to fight against religious bigotry and discrimination, including anti-Semitism?

Jesus struggled with religious people and structures

Questions for Lent

1. Imagine you meet a group of Pharisees feeling sore after an argument with Jesus; what advice would you offer to them?

2. The Jerusalem religious establishment could not imagine life without its Temple.
    a. Which structures do you consider integral to today's religious establishments?
    b. Which parts could you do without?
    c. Are there any parts to which might you feel overly attached? *And* can you imagine your outrage, should some upstart casually predict their destruction?

3. How easy is it to be distinctive by the quality of our love (as opposed to our costumes, churchgoing, religious busy-ness etc.)?

4. What different might being a 'professional Christian' make to someone's prayer life?

5. If you found yourself suddenly free from all duties and demands on your time, how would you observe the coming Holy Week and Easter?

PART FOUR

Jesus struggled with the crowds as the Kingdom dawned

Introduction – Jesus struggled with the crowds as the Kingdom dawned

'I came to bring fire to the earth, and how I wish it were already kindled!'
Luke 12:49

Watching a much-loved character turning completely evil was the least enjoyable thing about the final season of *Game of Thrones*. This person did not fundamentally change; their flaws were evident and carefully documented in the preceding seasons. Times and locations changed and together these permitted the flourishing of something we had chosen to ignore for seven whole seasons. This is where my discomfort lies. How had I persuaded myself to make such allowances for the earlier outbursts? I had heard this person making threats of appalling destruction, laying cities to waste and burning them to the ground. Instead of being alarmed, I chose to contextualise, excuse and then file away in a box labelled 'They're just upset. They don't mean it.' But I was wrong. They meant everything and the shock was breath taking. At least I never named a child after this 'hero'.

So now, as I read Jesus' words I feel a mixture of anxiety and confusion. He also states an intention to bring fire to the earth. We do not need to imagine what 'fire to the earth' looks like, we can see throughout history both invading and retreating armies destroying their enemies' cities; look at

Warsaw, Hiroshima and Aleppo. The horror ramps up to an unimaginable level when we try to imagine Jesus himself, kindling such destruction.

In the event he does nothing so literal. James and John are all for a bit of fiery devastation when a Samaritan village rejects them but Jesus rebukes them firmly.[137] When the time finally arrives for God to send fire from heaven, it comes in the form of life-giving Pentecostal courage.[138] Is this what Jesus means by bring 'fire to the earth'?

Perhaps he is talking about the refining of society by the burning of chaff or possibly the purifying of faith through persecution. Maybe he is referring to the last judgment. For now I will settle with the fact that God's Kingdom cannot be easily established. A struggle lies ahead. St Paul continues Jesus' line of thought, but takes a new metaphor from the maternity ward.

'We know that the whole creation has been groaning in labour pains until now' [139]

In this next section we see how this struggle unfolds as news of God's kingdom reaches crowds containing:

a.   rich people,
b.   excited people,
c.   people with fixed views about the Messiah
d.   people with fixed views about the scriptures
e.   people who get disillusioned and move on.

Jesus struggles with each of these groups.

There is an episode in *Game of Thrones* called 'The wars to come.'[140] Likewise we could call the days following Jesus' first proclamation of the Kingdom, 'The struggles to come'.

---

[137]   Luke 9:54-55.
[138]   Acts 2:1-4.
[139]   Romans 8:22.
[140]   *Game of Thrones*, HBO series, Season 5 Episode 1.

Day 1: Jesus struggled with the 'soft robes' crowd

'But woe to you who are rich, for you have received
your consolation.'

Luke 6:24

Jesus was clearly bothered by 'the rich' but more in principal than in person. He appears frustrated with their delusions and their wilful blindness. Maybe Jesus gets this from his mother who praises God for lifting up with poor, while sending the rich away empty handed.[141] God's Kingdom challenges them. They stand in stark contrast to the poor, for whom its dawning is unalloyed good news.

But try to find a rich person! By that I mean someone who willingly self-identifies as rich. Just try asking a random selection of people over the next couple of days if they are rich. You might get the following answers:

'Well we're not exactly poor but I certainly wouldn't call us rich.'

'Rich? You mean like the Beckhams? I wish.'

'I don't think so. And I've worked hard for everything I've got.'

---

[141] Luke 1:52-53.

'Seriously? With my bills? And prices rising all the time?'

'How about in global terms? Are you rich now?'

'Well of course, but you are too.'

My friend met me for a spin in his brand new customised Audi. So I asked him if he was rich. He baulked a bit but then allowed that possibly... he was 'doing okay'. Only when I re-phrased the question,

'How about in global terms? Are you rich now?'

he conceded,

'Well of course, but you are too.'

He is right. I am. There are several billion people on this planet who would willingly swap their financial situation with mine.

But why is admitting to wealth so uncomfortable, even from the heated driving seat of a new Audi? Maybe it is Jesus' fault. Have his criticisms of 'the rich' so seeped into our culture that we feel awkward in their ranks? Maybe we fear his rejection, forgetting that he sat at table with the rich as well as with the poor. Maybe it is part of being British; boasting about wealth is not quite the done thing ... when gently alluding to expensive tastes is much more acceptable. We joke. We self-deprecate. We look upwards, comparing ourselves only to those who are far, far wealthier. We protest the outrageous costs of everyday living whatever our income. In fact we will do almost anything to avoid naming our state, 'Hi, my name is ___ and I am rich.'

Poverty is real. There are a great many genuinely poor people in our world. There are also a considerable number who, not being as affluent as they would like, claim the status of 'poor'. It is as good a way as any of ducking the responsibilities of wealth, such as living with eyes, ears, hearts, hands (and wallets) open to those in need. Many who genuinely have less can be far more generous. I found a shocking fact in the *Financial Times*. Britain's ultra-rich (those with more than £10 million) give on average, £240 a year to charity. Only five percent of this group give more than 0.25 percent of their wealth each year.[142] Attitudes among the wealthy clearly have not changed much since Jesus observed a widow putting all she had into the Temple collection box.[143]

Jesus' threat to the rich is far more complex than simple doom. When he says, 'Woe to you who are rich' he could mean change, discomfort, awakening and upheaval but Jesus never wishes to see aristocratic necks on guillotines.

This becomes clear as his story unfolds.

He has meals with wealthy people and does not castigate them for their fortune.[144]

He himself depends on the bounty of others to fund his work; a group of affluent women including Joanna and Susanna get a special mention.[145]

Even after his death Jesus benefits from the generosity of Joseph of Arimathea, a man rich enough to have his own fully paid up burial plan.[146]

One of Gandhi's followers once made an illuminating comment: 'It costs an awful lot of money to keep Gandhiji living in poverty.' [147]

Gandhi did not give much thought to the expense of his hermitage. All such concerns were left for his wealthy supporters. There is no record of anyone saying anything similar about Jesus but hosting a wandering preacher with a minimum entourage of twelve males, has got to cost something.

None of this takes us away from the harsh words Jesus

---

[142] *Financial Times*, February 15 2019, 'Wealthy move to tackle pitiful state of UK philanthropy', Alice Ross, Wealth Correspondent.

[143] Mark 12:41-44, Luke 21:1-4.

[144] Luke 7:36-50, Luke 11:37.

[145] Luke 8:3.

[146] Matthew 27:57, Mark 15:43, Luke 23:50–56, John 19:39-40.

[147] *New York Times*, 6 February 1977, 'Mahatma Gandhi and His Apostles' by Paul Johnson.

has for the rich. In addition to his Lucan woes he lauds John the Baptist's example of righteousness comparing his living arrangements with those of the wealthy:

> 'What did you go out into the wilderness to look at? … Someone dressed in soft robes? Look, those who wear soft robes are in royal palaces.' [148]

The clear implication being that the 'soft robes' crowd are highly unlikely to be first to volunteer for service at the forefront of the Kingdom. Besides, riches tend to bloat egos beyond the size of camels, rendering them unable to pass through a narrow gate or the eye of a needle.[149]

Even more telling is Jesus' story of two men; one spends his days in opulence while the other, Lazarus, lies starving at his gate. In the next life, their roles are reversed. The rich man pleads for Abraham's help, but the answer comes back:

> 'Child, remember that during your lifetime you received your good things, and Lazarus in like manner evil things; but now he is comforted here, and you are in agony.'[150]

Behind this is a simple variant on Jesus' criticism of the Pharisees who do not lift a finger to assist those struggling with religious burdens.[151] Rich people run a much higher risk of focusing on property over people. Consequently they are less likely to step up when someone needs their aid. Elsewhere Jesus outlines the impossibility of serving both God and money.[152] We tell ourselves that we can find the balance but

---

[148] Matthew 11:8.
[149] Matthew 19:24, Mark 10:25 and Luke 18:25.
[150] Luke 16:25.
[151] Matthew 11:28-30.
[152] Matthew 6:24.

money has an unnerving ability to delude us, especially over where we stand on the rich/poor scale.

Alongside us

Rich or poor, Jesus draws alongside us. He sits at our tables and shares our food. If he has a go at us, it is less because we have wealth and more for what we do with it (and also what we let it do to us). He reminds us along with the rich fool[153] that nothing really belongs to us, so we are better off when we give more to God than to our bank vaults. The dawning Kingdom does not have to be bad news for the rich but in truth they, the 'soft robes' crowd are less likely to embrace its values than those with less to lose.

There are challenges ahead. If Jesus is bothered by the divide between rich and poor, we should be too. As he draws alongside us, do we share his reactions to a world split so deeply between the haves and have nots? It is easy to lampoon the delusions of a televangelist saying God needs him to have a new private jet,[154] but this might lead us to focus only on the extremes. Okay, I cannot deny that this level of wealth-fuelled stupidity is funny but it must not distract us for too long from our own responsibilities.

There are other serious pitfalls too. Good souls can become overwhelmed. There is the sad story of Olive Cooke, a generous, charitable woman and life-long poppy seller. At the age of 92 she tragically took her own life. At the time of her death she was receiving around 3000 mailings each year from different charities. Andrew Hind, as chair of the Fundraising Standards Board concluded,

---

[153] Luke 12:13-21.
[154] A BBC report dated 30 May 2018 tells how one Jesse Duplantis, an evangelist, believed that God had instructed him to buy a Falcon 7X costing £41m (his fourth private jet). Jesse overcame his initial hesitations when 'God' explained further, 'I didn't ask you to pay for it. I asked you to believe for it.'

'Her experience is a sad but extremely important case as it sheds light on the way in which fundraising activity could escalate and leave a committed donor feeling under pressure to give.'[155]

If we are to venture more deeply into the world of giving we cannot do so without guidance, lest the ocean of need deluges our flame of hope. As well as over-eager charities, there are fraudsters out there who will fleece every penny from generous souls. I know Jesus tells us to give without letting our left hand know what the right is doing, but it is always wise to find a trusted friend who can talk us through any concerns about escalating demands, especially those which come from 'unofficial' sources.

Loving God draw alongside us,
close enough for our hearts to learn your challenges
close enough to allow your light into
both our wallets and our delusions
close enough for us to hear, as you do,
the cry of the poor
close enough to hear your guidance on how best to respond
and how never to separate wisdom from kindness. **AMEN**

---

[155] The *Guardian*, 20 January 2016, 'Poppy seller who killed herself got 3,000 charity requests for donations a year', Steven Morris.

Day 2: Jesus struggled with the excited crowd

When they found him on the other side of the lake,
they said to him, 'Rabbi, when did you come here?' Jesus
answered them, 'Very truly, I tell you, you are looking
for me, not because you saw signs, but because you
ate your fill of the loaves.'
John 6:25-26

Imagine a pair of tourists who have travelled to Agra in India and are now following signposts to the Taj Mahal. They reach the final signpost, which points to an archway. Through this they will find one of the most glorious buildings on the planet. They stop, overwhelmed with excitement. They take selfies with this final signpost behind them. They post these online. Their pictures capture their moment to perfection, their wide-eyed anticipation and their perfect smiles. Immediately their timelines start to fill with comments, which they pause to answer.

'Can't believe you guys made it!'

'Yep, it's incredible. This is it! We've arrived!'

Only they have not arrived and they never do, because by the time they have finished updating their social media accounts and replying to each of their friends, the gates have shut for the night. And at dawn their tour bus leaves for Varanasi.

Okay, this is an unlikely story and I invented it to illustrate the ridiculousness of getting too excited about a sign and missing the attraction itself. However it might not be so far from reality ... I once took a trip from Delhi to Kathmandu. When we finally arrived, my husband announced: 'I'm going to climb the steps to the Monkey Temple. Anyone fancy joining me?'

This put two of our group into a quandary, it was after all a bit of hike from our hotel and we only had the morning before we flew back home.

'We might,' they said, 'but we're also thinking about finding somewhere to get our nails done.'

Likewise, the crowds who flock to Jesus often miss the point. He is the latest thing and everyone wants a slice. Nowadays the crowds would insist on photos, hashtagged with #SelfiesWithTheSaviour. Back then, they could only enjoy the fireworks in real time. Anticipation runs high, bolstered by stories of:

- water turned into wine,
- deaf people hearing,
- blind people seeing,
- those who had never walked, dancing and
- thousands enjoying a free meal that starts with just one lad's picnic lunch.

Crazy theories abound about just how Jesus manages to cross from one side of the sea of Galilee to the other without a boat. Who would not queue up to witness something this spectacular?

This is the risk Jesus takes whenever he signals the dawning of God's Kingdom by performing miracles. The crowds get so wowed by the signs that they neglect to look at where they are pointing. One day Jesus speaks out. We can guess that he is struggling with a bit of frustration because he pronounces a couple of 'woes'. The first goes to the towns of Chorazin and Bethsaida. Jesus puts it to them that the gentile towns of Tyre and Sidon would have repented quickly and sincerely, had they seen the same signs. Capernaum is next in the firing line. This town has likewise failed to understand the meaning behind Jesus' acts of power. In fact Capernaum messes up so badly that Jesus relegates it to somewhere behind Sodom in the stakes for judgement day.[156]

As Jesus does these wonderful things, the hoped-for response is something more than the superficial ooos and ahs of a firework display. He wants the crowds to stop all their non-Kingdom activities, recognise their non-Kingdom mind-sets, do a 180 turn around, start thinking Kingdomwise and start walking Kingdomwards back to God … or as he puts it 'repent'.

This is a frustrating struggle for Jesus. He puts in some long shifts, with early starts and late finishes. The needs of the crowds are huge and his compassion often deprives him of rest breaks. Should we be surprised that the crowds sometimes wind him up, especially when in their excitement, they completely miss his point?

There is a contemporary parallel as Greta Thunberg travels around addressing august bodies such as the US Congress. She insists emphatically that her speeches and the school strikes are *not* be praised. If Congress is appreciative, they should redirect their attention the climate scientists. Her protests, like Jesus' miracles exist as signposts, which should not detain admirers for too long. The analogy breaks down beyond this point; whereas Greta Thunberg is adamant that people should look beyond her, Jesus invites the crowds to look *more intently* at what he does and thus understand who he is.

Alongside us

We cannot control what others make of us. People will often make negative, over-positive or wildly-inaccurate assessments about who we are and why we do things. Until we can develop a workable Jedi mind trick we have no way of preventing this.

[156] Matthew 11:20-24.

If we begin to protest we run the risk of protesting too much.

One of the quirks of preaching comes in that moment when someone says,

'I can so clearly remember you saying in one of your sermons...'

... followed by something I cannot conceive ever having said.

This is far worse for people caught in the media's spotlight, who have almost no control over how they are portrayed to the world.

Reality TV creates drama though careful editing. Only after they have left the goldfish bowl, do some contestants learn that they have been the villain of a series. All their cattiest comments and laziest moments have been broadcast with all their redeeming qualities excised. I can understand why TV does this; everyone-getting-along-splendidly is hardly a ratings winner but the cost to the individuals and their families can huge. And all because the media loves a sensation. And the sad fact is villainous 'sensations' are easier to market than virtuous ones.

The point is Jesus could not control how the crowds thought even when he was doing his most crowd-pleasing things. He therefore knows the frustration of being misunderstood and misrepresented. He struggled because despite all his sacrifices of time, love, wisdom and energy, the crowds often resisted following his signs and turning towards God's Kingdom.

Loving Jesus, come alongside us,
into our multi-platformed lives.
We see how you struggled to make yourself understood
and how you were so often unsuccessful.
Warm us by your breath
and make us the exceptions.
Make us the ones,
who are continually turning back to you,
and finding new delight,
in the goodness of your ways. **AMEN**

Day 3: Jesus struggled with the expectant crowd

And their eyes were opened. Then Jesus sternly ordered them, 'See that no one knows of this.'
Matthew 9:30

I wonder how many vicars and church wardens have looked in bemusement at a stack of tins following a harvest festival. Some can be dealt with easily. These come from the people who actually read the requests in the church magazine and donate accordingly.

Other tins prompt responses such as:

'How on earth would you cook this?'

'Have you seen the best before date? Our Danny was still in primary school when this went off.'

and,

'I didn't even know you could get this in tins.'

Some people clearly use harvest as an excuse to clear out the deeper recesses of their cupboards.

The most intriguing tins are those without labels. They provide a fun game akin to Russian roulette for anyone who hates throwing food away. An unlabelled tin of beans looks identical to an unlabelled tin of dog food. I would open one up from time to time, not knowing if I would find soup, chickpeas or out-of-date Tip Top. This is the value of labels. Labels tell us what to expect inside.

They are essential for tins but less so for humans. When

applied to us labels can be both useful *and* misleading. On learning that someone bears a label such as nurse, trans, atheist, former-prisoner, Brummie, Buddhist, rough-sleeper, mountaineer, Conservative or hunt saboteur, we invariably make a series of assumptions, only some of which will prove accurate.

Jesus seems okay with labels such as Rabbi, Teacher, Lord, Son of David, healer and prophet. He even coins one for himself, the intriguing 'Son of Man'. During his time as a wandering preacher the one label he is most keen to avoid is 'Messiah'. He foresees that if too many people stick this label on him, he will be forever fighting all number of accompanying erroneous expectations.

He is proved right in this. His twelve, or at least Peter (speaking for all of them) identifies him as the Messiah.[157] Jesus congratulates him and then immediately forbids any repetition of this in public hearing.[158] Even so, the label 'Messiah' proves tricky; the twelve cannot see the difference between Jesus and their longed-for warrior 'Messiah', ridding the land of Romans and restoring Jewish rule.[159] And if the twelve who live cheek by jowl with Jesus struggle with this, what chance do the wider population have?

How could the crowds ever appreciate him at face-value if their minds are already fizzing with 'messianic' expectation? If news of this label gets out, Jesus' conversations might not past a constant repetition of, 'Yes, but not *that* sort of messiah!'

Added to this, the Romans and Herod take a dim view of wannabe messiahs and tend to remove them permanently from public circulation. So Jesus decides his wisest course is to play down the label wherever possible.

To this end, Jesus often orders people to keep shtum about his acts.

---

[157] Matthew 16:16.
[158] Matthew 16:20, Mark 8:29-30, Luke 9:21.
[159] Acts 1:6. for more on this see Chapter 2 (d).

He sternly warns a newly healed leper to say nothing (but to no avail).[160]

He likewise silences unclean spirits.[161]

and his disciples (again) after his Transfiguration.[162]

Despite Jesus' oft-noted firmness, his tactic is not successful. Also he does not apply his 'messianic secret' consistently. Jesus performs other miracles, including healings without making any such strictures.

The crowds, even without being given the 'messiah' label, draw their own conclusions. Left to their own devices they would set him up on a makeshift throne and force a tin crown onto his head. In John's Gospel, we read,

> 'When the people saw the sign that he had done, they began to say, 'This is indeed the prophet who is to come into the world.' When Jesus realised that they were about to come and take him by force to make him king, he withdrew again to the mountain by himself.'[163]

So Jesus is caught in a difficult situation. How can he continue his ministry without generating these kind of expectations? How can he proclaim God's Kingdom without people imagining him as their future king? Should he disappear for a while to allow the rumours to die down? How about restraining his compassion and not healing the sick? Maybe he can do a Ratner[164] and shatter his reputation? Ridiculous as that sounds, in the end he does choose a path that leads to derision. There are those who will always view the crucified as

---

[160] Mark 1:43-45 (see also Matthew 8:4, Luke 5:14).

[161] Mark 1:25 & 3:11-12 (see also Luke 4:33-35 and Matthew 12:15-16).

[162] Matthew 17:9, Mark 9:9.

[163] John 6:14-15.

[164] Gerald Ratner famously sabotaged the reputation of his own jewellery business by publicly declaring his shops sold 'total crap'.

failure as cursed by God.[165] Many still believe the thorns are his final crown.

His best way forward is to attempt rumour control. This is a struggle, as he knows it will never be watertight, but still it is better than doing nothing.

Alongside us

Once again we return to this truth; we have limited control over what others think of us. We might dispute the labels they stick on us but we can neither forbid them nor successfully remove all of them. We might try to protect our identity - our sense of self, with secrets but these are rarely safe. Benjamin Franklin once quipped: 'Three may keep a secret, if two of them are dead.'

The moment we forbid someone to pass on a piece of information we set up a circle of privilege that intrigues others. Once we had learnt that a Chamber of Secrets exists, we know Harry Potter will find it. He has to. The title demands it. Presumably, the name of the shop 'Victoria's Secret' was chosen with the same reasoning; the fact that she has a secret creates a curiosity that will only be satisfied by a visit.

The more we try to disguise a secret the more prominent it becomes. Chilled by George Orwell's *1984*, we once feared the ransacking of our secrets. Now we serve up our private lives to the world on the platters of social media but are still astonished whenever the rats come to bite us.

We are frequently told 'to be ourselves' but with very little guidance as to how. We are left wondering who we really are and which of our labels are accurate. Are we:

- our professional selves?
- one of our online personas?
- the person people say we are?
- the person whose self-esteem depends on their number of daily 'likes'?

[165] Galatians 3:13.

I have heard of an extreme disease where people become jealous of the life they themselves lead on Instagram, whose retouched pictures are simply better than their everyday reality.

I remain convinced that the best way I can 'be myself' is to find who I am in God's eyes. That happens most frequently when I am aware of Jesus alongside me. He makes sense of the labels that God offers to us, labels that are both long-lasting and worthwhile; God labels us as:

- chosen
- royal
- holy, and
- 'God's own'

… at least according to Peter.[166]

> Jesus in this world,
> where control is more illusory than real,
> where our secrets can so easily be uncovered,
> where labels can be posted on us without our asking,
> draw alongside us and,
> help to find that
> our place alongside you is identity enough,
> whatever anyone else says. **AMEN**

[166] 1 Peter 2:9.

Day 4: Jesus struggled with the scripturally-minded crowd (and with the scriptures)

Jesus answered them, 'You are wrong, because you know neither the scriptures nor the power of God.'
Matthew 22:29

Can you imagine anyone having the same reaction to Jesus as to Donald Trump? (If you are a fan of the latter, well done for getting this far in the book but I suspect what follows will not delight you.) Most Brits that I know take a dim view of the 45th US President, greeting his statements with a shake of the head and something along the lines of,

'I can't believe he just said that!'

'How can he not see how wrong he is?'

And,

'How dare he!'

Take that reaction and now transfer it to someone in a crowd, listening to Jesus ... because Jesus speaks with a similar level of staggering presumption. Matthew in particular, remembers a formula that Jesus employs in variants of, 'It was said in ancient times, but I say to you ...' [167]

Several in the crowd start feeling very uncomfortable,

'Did he really say that? Is he seriously standing there and

[167] Matthew 5:22, 5:28, 5:32, 5:34, 5:39, 5:44 and 19:9.

expecting us to accord *his* teaching precedence over the *Law of Moses?'*

In Jesus we see either an arrogance of megalomaniac proportions or the calmly stated end-result of a titanic struggle. We do not hear anything about how Jesus wrestled with the scriptures but we do get to read his post-struggle conclusions. We can guess at what he was given as a child and then contrast it with what he says as an adult. Somewhere in between these two, lies a radical re-evaluation.

If Jesus made any of his statements off the cuff and without hours of agonised, soul-searching struggle, he could be likened to a politician brandishing preposterous claims ... the sort of claims that shatter under the most facile interrogation. Donald Trump, for instance is on record as saying,

'I was the most transparent, and am, transparent President in history'[168]

'I am the most popular person in the history of the Republican Party'[169]

'I'm very highly educated. I know words, I have the best words'[170]

'I am the least racist person you have ever interviewed, that I can tell you'[171]

'I cherish women. I want to help women. I'm going to be able to do things for women that no other candidate would be able to do.'[172]

[168] CNN May 25, 2019 *'Fact-checking Trump claims he's 'the most transparent' president in US history'* By Marshall Cohen and Holmes Lybrand, CNN.
[169] Quoted from an interview in The Sun by Olivia Ovenden in *Esquire*, July 13, 2018.
[170] Donald Trump during a public speech, easily found on YouTube.
[171] Donald Trump in answer to a question from John King, CNN Anchor, January 15, 2018.
[172] Donald Trump, quoted in 'Donald Trump: all the sexist things he said', Adam Lusher in The *Independent*, 9 October 2016

'Believe it or not, I watch my words very carefully. There are those that think I'm a very stable genius.'[173]

There are many more but I need to stop otherwise this chapter risks a new title … *The 'I am' sayings of Donald Trump.*

Okay there is a final one I could not resist,

'I think I'm much more humble than you would understand.'[174]

His grandiose boasts are often deflated not by his opponents but by he himself with *his own words*![175] My point (aside from enjoying an all too easy jibe) is very serious. Jesus makes claims that to opponents, might sound as outrageous as those made by Donald Trump. The difference between the two men is as the gulf that separates Lazarus from Dives. Jesus lived a consistent life and his integrity bore up under intense scrutiny. In short Jesus was worthy of making such claims and not least because he did his rigorous homework before opening his mouth on a public platform.

What this 'homework' looks like, we can only guess but it surely involved some considerable struggles. It takes courage to question the fundamental rules that are woven into the fabric of everyday life. An old Chinese proverb says: 'If you want to know what water is like don't ask a fish.'

We can adapt this to: 'If you want to know how to improve on age old laws, don't ask a guy who has grown up knowing nothing else.'

But there is no record of Jesus travelling away from the Holy Land, apart from a short stint in Egypt when he was a

---

[173] From a joint press conference with Finnish President Sauli Niinistö, in answer to a question from Reuters journalist Jeff Mason, quoted in the *Guardian* October 3, 2019 *Donald Trump's bizarre press day was a full-blown impeachment tantrum* by David Smith

[174] Donald Trump in an interview with Eric Stahl on *60 Minutes* 2018, widely quoted and viewable on YouTube.

[175] There is no starker example than his 'locker room' chat about grabbing women 'by the pussy'… something he feels clearly entitled to do … because he is a star.

baby. In his younger life, he does not go off on a gap year to expand his mind and then return home, brimming with fresh perspectives. So we must conclude that his questioning powers were immense. His impressive travels are all in his mind, fuelled by prayer, reading, study and debate (and we know he is an early starter with this).[176]

Somewhere behind his bold statements lies an immense struggle with the scriptures. How long did it take him to imagine something better than Moses' proposal for limiting revenge?[177]

> You have heard that it was said, 'An eye for an eye and a tooth for a tooth.' But I say to you, Do not resist an evildoer. But if anyone strikes you on the right cheek, turn the other also.[178]

Gandhi also saw the flaw with Moses' way and said,

> 'An eye for an eye only ends up making the whole world blind'

But then Gandhi grew up in a very different time and culture. He was also building on Jesus' teaching, rather than coming up, as Jesus did, with something entirely new.

John's Gospel remembers another of Jesus' sermon hooks, his 'I am' sayings.[179] These also are highly controversial as Jesus awards himself roles and titles far beyond the claim of any other human. He courts further outrage by echoing,

> 'I AM who I AM.'

[176] Luke 2:41-52
[177] Leviticus 24:19-20
[178] Matthew 5:38-39
[179] John 6:48 I am the bread of life, 8:12 the light of the world, 10:7 the gate for the sheep, 10:11 the good shepherd, 11:25 the resurrection and the life, 14:6 the way, the truth and life, 15:2 the true vine.

the holy name God revealed to Moses at the burning bush.[180] At what point, in his struggles with scripture, did Jesus decide it would be appropriate to adapt these words and apply them to himself?

Unsurprisingly many in the crowd find Jesus extremely offensive. And whilst we do not witness him struggling with the scriptures, we see both the fruit of those struggles and his subsequent struggles with those who deride him as blasphemous.

Alongside us

I try my hardest not engage in Twitter spats. My rule is that I will not answer anyone who hides behind an obvious pseudonym. Sometimes I slip up and before I know it I find myself locked into an exchange. My downfall is usually a hooked tweet, baited with something dumb but easy-to-fix about religion and sexuality. The ensuing argument inevitably boils down to differing interpretations of scripture. I get accused of distorting God-given texts purely to suit my own perverse ends. I try to dress up my reply into something more polite but it boils down to pretty much the same and so the night wears on.

This game was a favourite in theological college (only we had to play it face-to-face as this was pre-Twitter). A group of hardliners would end each of their statements with accusations such as, 'Can't you see? You're flying in the face of Scripture?'

Then, the best I muster was a flustered and wholly inadequate, 'No I'm not!'

But now I want to point out how Jesus did far more than reinterpret scripture. He updated scripture and at times he rewrote scripture.

Of course, I want to take the Old Testament very seriously but it is not Gospel. Neither quotes from Leviticus nor stories about Sodom and Gomorrah hold equal weight with the

[180] Exodus 3:1-15.

teaching of Jesus. And Jesus is the person I want, more than any other, alongside me as I read scripture today.

On a side note I read with interest a tweet from President Donald Trump himself.

'Numerous states introducing Bible Literacy classes, giving students the option of studying the Bible. Starting to make a turn back? Great!'[181]

I am all for greater access to the Bible, provided it is never forced on anyone. But I wonder why *this* President is so keen for young people to engage with scripture and risk the possibility of meeting Jesus ... since Jesus shows such radical respect for women, such deep concern for the poor, and such generous welcome for the stranger and outcast. Surely this exercise risks leading young people into their own struggles against his policies?

Loving Jesus,
your treatment of scripture outrages some,
and yet to many more it gives peace
beyond understanding.
Please sit alongside us as we read today.
Help us as we struggle to connect
ancient wisdom with modern dilemmas.
Keep us from weaponising verses.
Instead meet us and inspire us,
to acts of love and worship. **AMEN**

---

[181] Twitter 28 Jan 2019 – 1.21 PM @realDonaldTrump.

Day 5: Jesus struggled with the departing crowd

Because of this many of his disciples turned back and no longer went about with him. So Jesus asked the twelve, 'Do you also wish to go away?'
John 6:66-67

Spotify has opened my eyes as well as my ears. I have discovered to my astonished amazement that many of my favourite bands from the 1980s still exist and unbeknownst to me are still recording music. Take Erasure; I never stopped liking them. There was never one single moment when I decided to ignore them but over a period, new fresher acts burst onto the scene and drew my attention away. Back in the day, I knew exactly when their next album was due for release. Now in 2019 a few mouse-clicks suddenly reveal a further twelve Erasure albums that are completely new to me. The point is that popular culture shifted its spotlight away from them … and I blithely - even sheepishly - followed.

I am guessing that many people in the crowds once so enthusiastic about Jesus, make a similar journey. The saying goes that you are only as good as your last hit. The crowd loves Jesus' back catalogue of stories and miracles but his new material bombs; his speech conflating eating bread with eating his flesh is a notable low point, at least for the majority of the crowd. They find it confusing, hard to swallow and frankly a bit gross. It lacks the catchiness of his earlier work and many of them simply wander off looking for the next new thing.

Jesus next question sounds sad. He turns to the twelve and asks if they too plan to leave. Simon Peter asks where else they would go, since they still believe he has the words of eternal life. This must be reassuring for Jesus but maybe not enough to counteract the pain of rejection. Jesus' huge popularity is always a mixed blessing but this swift descent from being deified to discarded would be hard for anyone, so why not for Jesus too? Desertion hurts.

There are not enough lines of dialogue here, for us to read between them with any great hope of reaching accurate conclusions. We cannot truly see how Jesus is feeling. However it might be telling that his next recorded words are less than cheerful. He reminds the remaining twelve that it was he who chose them and *not* the other way around. And *then,* he lobs a bomb into their midst. He tells them that one of them is a devil.

Comments like that do not come from a happy place and I imagine the twelve spending the rest of that day coping with many anxious questions,

'Who did he mean by *that*?'

'What? One of us is a devil?'

'Was he serious?'

'He said *a* devil not *the* devil, right?'

'Well I have my suspicions as to who he m … but horrors, suppose he meant me?'

We could get carried away with guesswork here. John ends this episode and quickly moves on. Jesus returns to Galilee, finding Judea too hot for comfort. I am still left wondering whether any of the twelve come back to Jesus for clarification later on or if they all silently agree that it is best not to, as clearly he is not having a good day.

Moving deeper into the uncertain and unfathomable realms of speculation, I wonder what Jesus' own prayers are like that evening. How does he bring himself to God? Does he use words?

Does he lament? Does he pray for his anxious disciples? Even with no possibility of answers, the questions still intrigue me.

Alongside us

Very few people linger long in the media spotlight. A few sports players get a second career as pundits and somehow the Stones keep on rolling, but they are exceptions. Today's stars are mostly tomorrow's has-beens. Many bands from the 1980s need to club together to fill venues smaller than those where they once headlined. This loss of status is not just the preserve of the stars. Most of us will struggle with a sense declining power as we go through life.

A newly retired fire fighter once said to me,

'I still get up at five thirty every morning, just because I always have. I have my breakfast. My wife goes out to work and I leave with her to walk the dog. Then I come back home and do all the housework. I make myself a cup of tea and look at the clock. It's only nine-thirty. From then onwards I don't know what to do with myself so I count down the hours until she returns at teatime.'

As we talked further it became clear that the fire service had always been more than a job to him, it had been his status, his pre-set timetable and his entire social life. He had never needed to go out and make friends. All the friends he could ever want were at the station, their camaraderie cemented by the intensity of their work. He was very much in the *'used to be'* stage in life; if someone were to ask, 'And what do you do?' his answer would be, 'I *used to be* a fireman.'

He is not the only one to face this struggle.

- Parents become empty nesters.
- The newly retired A&E nurse wakes one day to find no queue of people awaiting their expertise.

- Retail workers are made redundant as yet another high-street chain falls victim to the online giants.
- The former executive snaps at their partner, 'I'm used to things getting done when I ask for them'
- The elderly person tries to make their single room feel a bit more like the house in which they can no longer safely stay.

And so on. Stories of declining power are all around us.

Vicars can attend every course going on church growth. They can battle against the perennial 'but this is the way things have always been done here' to produce something more attractive for the people who do not yet attend. But the sad reality is a story of decreasing numbers attending services. The Church of England's traditional power will not be worth beans if the day comes when all its pews are empty. Concerned Anglicans can feel as helpless as Canute, only for him the tide was rising; for us it seems to be ebbing away.

Jesus never reached retirement. His death came before the aches and unreliable joints of old age. He never had to close a crumbling Victorian church whilst struggling to support its bereaved members. However he gained a taste of these complicated feelings on the day the crowds wandered off. His brush with *'used to be'* ('I *used to be* far more popular') gives him a personal experience of something most of us will struggle with, as our lives progress.

> Jesus guide us to accept with your grace
> the loss of temporary powers.
> Keep us from clinging too fondly
> to that which was only briefly ours.
> Direct us instead to the now
> and to this day's good invitations.
> And console us the truth that,
> with you alongside us,
> we will never be truly deserted. **AMEN**

Days 6 and 7: Jesus struggled with the crowds as the kingdom dawned ... some concluding thoughts

The crowds are a mixed bag. They are the cause of much frustration for Jesus. Like the twelve, they do not share his values, they often miss his point entirely, they consider him as disposable as any other form of entertainment and they want to turn him into something he is not. So given this level of hassle ... why does Jesus bother with the crowds at all?

My first introductions to Jesus focused so strongly on his sacrificial death as to virtually eclipse everything else. My view of salvation expanded in time to encompass his birth and resurrection but even at this stage, had I been asked, 'Why does he spends so much time with the crowds?' I would have had no ready answer. Surely God's salvation plan just required him to die for us? Jesus could live as a hermit, supported by a small core group of devoted followers. He would still need to be arrested and executed but that could be achieved by the donkey ride, the table turning and a few choice comments about destroying the Temple. After all, the Romans are hardly reticent when it comes to terminating threats to their fragile pax.

So why does he spend three years out and about with the crowds, knowing that so many would never 'get' him? And if this question seems preposterous, consider the great Christian creeds. They completely excise his public ministry from their mini-biographies. The Apostles' Creed rushes him straight from being born of the Virgin Mary to suffering under Pontius Pilate, with no mention of his teaching, healing, delivering or personal example. He fares no better in the Chalcedonian, Athanasian or Nicene versions. It is as if all his interactions with the crowds are irrelevant to the great work of salvation. And yet his three years out on the road are clearly important for him, otherwise why would he struggle on (rather than seek out a hermit's cave)?

Perhaps we, by which I mean the crowds then and us today, need the stories generated by Jesus' public ministry. We could be given the simple words, 'God is love' and we could be told that 'God so loved the world ...', but we need this to be fleshed out. Humans are a story-loving species. We would be far less interested in theological formulae if these were presented apart from the tales of wind, waves, wells, lepers, loaves, fishes, Pharisees, parables and panicked pigs.

Jesus wants to give the crowds a living demonstration of God's Kingdom. Salvation is far more than the afterlife. We need his teaching if we want to imagine the Kingdom here on earth as well as in heaven.

Moreover, Jesus' interactions with the crowds reveal God's nature, not as some easily-piqued tyrant but as a loving, forgiving Abba who is constantly compelled by compassion. Jesus' living among us shows us what divine love looks like in a very human form. Goodness knows what number of bizarre theories we might concoct around his birth, death and resurrection without this wider context.

Perhaps he could have achieved our salvation as a hermit but I remain profoundly grateful for all his struggles with the crowds. The stories from then are the ones that show how, even today he can be alongside us.

Jesus struggled with the crowds as the Kingdom dawned

Questions for any time of year

1. Do you agree with the assessment *Jesus was clearly bothered by "the rich" but more in principle than in person*? If so was he inconsistent?
   a. What would a Jesus who was harsher with the rich look like?
   b. Are you rich?

2. Do you have a greater sense of Jesus alongside you when you are part of large crowd, in a small group or on your own?

3. Jesus accepted certain labels (he even coined one for himself), but sought to avoid the label 'Messiah', at least until the time was right.
   a. Do you find labels helpful?
   b. Which ones?
   c. And which ones less so?

4. How good would you have been at keeping Jesus' identity secret, had you been healed by him?

5. Given the amount of hassle the crowds brought Jesus, why do you think he spent so much time trying to engage meaningfully with them?

Jesus struggled with the crowds as the Kingdom dawned

Questions for Advent

1. 'What can I give him, poor as I am?' [182] Christina Rosetti's answer, 'Give him my heart', is of course the prime answer. However it is not the only one; Jesus of Nazareth benefitted from the generous material resources of others.
   a. What material resources does he need most now?
   b. What material resource can you offer him today?

2. Christmas is a time of immense peer pressure, to do, to perform, to purchase and to sparkle along with everyone else. How does Jesus' resistance to public expectations inform your choices this season?

3. Thinking about how Jesus did not use the term 'Messiah' openly:
   a. Do you see any differences between someone having a private life, a secret life and a double life?
   b. How does Jesus living alongside us help us to live honestly and with integrity?

4. As you approach the turning of another year, do you reflect on loss of status, perhaps through redundancy or retirement? How do you imagine Jesus can be alongside you in a future where you are not able to do so much?

---

[182] 'In the Bleak Midwinter', Christina Rossetti, 1872.

Jesus struggled with the crowds as the Kingdom dawned

Questions for Lent

1. Thinking of my sports car-driving friend who was so resistant of the 'rich tag'...
   a. Do you consider yourself rich, poor or somewhere in between?
   b. How much would you need to possess before you would accept for yourself the 'rich tag'?
   c. And what would change for you if you owned that tag?

2. How do you define the word 'repent'?
   a. What associations does it hold for you?
   b. How does it sound when spoken by Jesus?

3. Studying the scriptures is a key Lenten discipline.
   a. How different does the Old Testament look when read alongside Jesus' teaching and example?
   b. What sort of 'homework' did Jesus do with the scriptures before speaking in public?
   c. Can you empathise with those who took offence at the fruit of Jesus' struggle to reinterpret scripture?

4. Can you find Jesus alongside you when nothing seems to be going well and nothing you do succeeds?

PART FIVE

Jesus was NOT troubled by many of the things that stress us

Introduction – Jesus was NOT troubled by many of the things that stress us

We are going to take a break from Jesus' difficulties and have a think about some of the things that did not stress Jesus. This book deliberately focuses on his struggles and therefore needs an occasional reminder that he is not defined solely by his hardships. I have added the following reflections to offer some balance lest I present Jesus solely as a grim-faced, resolute figure, so caught up in his multitude of struggles that he has little energy left to crack a smile.

My former colleague, the Revd Jo Calladine often runs a discussion group in the prison, where she lays out pictures of Jesus and asks the residents to pick the one to which they are most drawn. Their choices are often revealing. Many opt for a Victorian image of a blondish Jesus who appears gentle, kind and inoffensive. He sits in a pastel setting surrounded by small animals. This was my least favourite but perhaps it evokes memories for them of more innocent days. And maybe childhood was the last time some of them sat down to talk about Jesus. Jo's favourite is always an image of Jesus laughing. She sees him as someone with an attractive personality, whose natural warmth draws in people. She imagines him as both jovial and engaging, concluding that, surely, he is great company.

I am convinced she is right. I am equally certain that the

stories we are examining elsewhere in this book, are less likely to show this side of him. To counter this I would like us to consider some of the everyday stresses that find no purchase in him. He clearly has an enviable skill for sitting light to much that drags the rest of us down.

An estimated 595,000 of us in the UK, suffered from work-related stress in 2017-18, a rise from the previous year's figure of 526,000. Statistics show that 57 per cent of lost working days were due to stress.[183] This is either a growing problem or something that we are only just starting to acknowledge. Either way we need help.

Jesus certainly never spends the final day of a holiday dreading the 1,000 emails that he will find in his inbox on Monday morning. And when he goes to the synagogue, he never needs to switch his phone to silent. There are many more modern-day stresses that he does not experience. However this should not disqualify him as our guide to a healthier way of life and a good companion for our journey.

We begin with a very current problem, our overriding anxiety about our reputations …

---

[183] Figures taken from bbc.co.uk, 5 December 2018, *'How do you tackle stress in the workplace?'*, Hugh Pym (Health Editor).

Day 1: Jesus was not troubled by his reputation (and the people who might sully it)

'This fellow welcomes sinners and eats with them.'
Luke 15:2b

Compare Jesus with the modern 'influencer'. For the latter reputation is everything. They spend most of their energy polishing themselves to the kind of dazzling sheen that attracts new advertisers and keeps investors on board. They build immaculate online presences, saying all the right things in the right places whilst wearing the right clothes.

Jessica and Garrett Gee make their fortune through YouTube and other social media platforms. They call themselves the 'Bucket List Family'. They travel the world with their three children, shooting short films of themselves enjoying the most enviable experiences. These rack up millions of views, so it is no surprise that hotels and resorts line up to welcome them (and their cameras). When their hundreds and thousands of subscribers see how much family-friendly-fun a destination offers, they reach for the nearest mouse and start booking. The three Gee children all have their own Instagram accounts (managed by their parents). The youngest, Calihan, a toddler at the time of writing, already has 295,000 followers. And that is the bottom line for the advertisers. No one would be interested in them if no one else was watching them, but as it is every vlog they post is seen by a huge audience. Who would not want to watch young Calihan learning to take his first unsteady steps surrounded by wobbly penguins on a windswept beach in the Falkland Islands? It all adds to their reputation as a wholesome, caring, adventurous family. And as their financial success depends entirely on this reputation, we get to see more of the sunshine-cute moments and less of the tantrums in the rain.

Jesus in contrast pays scant regard to his reputation. He makes some very poor choices, almost to the point of sabotage. He shows a blithe disregard for the expectations of his peers as he mixes with all the wrong people in all the wrong places. If his opponents had access to social media they would post images of him chatting with prostitutes, gentiles, Roman centurions, Samaritan women, Syro-Phoenician women, tax-collectors and various assorted sinners, tagging them with #drunkard #glutton #WeKnewAllAlong and #DontBeFooled.[184]

Did he not know how dangerous this was even without social media's beady eye? Some six hundred years before Jesus' birth, Aesop said, 'A man is known by the company he keeps.' Had this wisdom failed to reach the Holy Land or did Jesus simply have different priorities?

Will Storr argues that reputation is key to human beings.[185] This lesson was learnt in our days as hunter gatherers. Our ancestors are the ones who made good choices about how the rest of the tribe perceived them. They have bequeathed to us an inbuilt 'hard-wired' anxiety about our status within our tribe.

How does Jesus manage to be so unconcerned about his reputation? Take the occasion when Jesus is the guest of Simon the Pharisee; a woman turns up and she is … well, Luke does not go into specific detail here, but her reputation

---

[184] See Matthew 11:19, Luke 7:34.
[185] *'Selfie: How The West Became Self-Obsessed'* (Book 1; The Tribal Self), Will Storr (Picador 2017).

is 'a woman in the city, who was a sinner'.[186] She gate-crashes the party and makes an embarrassing show of herself, crying, carrying on and clinging to Jesus' feet.

This is not quite the spectacle Simon was planning. In those days poorer folk were allowed to enter the homes of the rich, to observe the powerful at play, much as we might watch vlogs of celebrities on holiday. There were rules then as now; the poor are certainly not permitted to break rank and actually engage with any person of consequence. This woman breaks convention, which is bad enough, but Jesus' behaviour is arguably worse. Far from recoiling in disgust, he seems to encourage her.

Simon should be outraged but I suspect he is almost grateful for this intrusive woman. After all she is proving everything that he has long suspected about this Nazarene upstart. He says to himself.

'If this man were a prophet, he would have known who and what kind of woman this is who is touching him— that she is a sinner.'[187]

Jesus overhears and his reply is magnificent. He stumps Simon with the parable of the two debtors ... A creditor is owed money by two people. One owes considerably more than the other. The creditor cancels both of their debts. The one forgiven the far larger debt is far more grateful. Jesus then returns his attention to Simon and gesturing to the woman concludes:

'Therefore, I tell you, her sins, which were many, have been forgiven; hence she has shown great love. But the one to whom little is forgiven, loves little.' [188]

Simon (and the rest of us) have much to learn about the dynamics of God's forgiveness.

[186] Luke 7:37.
[187] Luke 7:39.
[188] Luke 7:47.

On another occasion a different group of Pharisees and Scribes take a pop at Jesus for eating with undesirables [189]. He responds with three parables: the lost sheep, the lost coin and most joyously, the lost sons [190]. Kenneth Bailey argues that this third parable is structurally incomplete [191]. There is a missing final stanza. The younger brother returns and accepts the father's welcome. The elder brother, the supposedly good one, remains outside, seething with resentment. His father leaves his guests and comes outside to persuade his eldest to join him... And the parable ends here.

We expect a resolution but Jesus fails to supply one. There is no, 'And they began to celebrate' following on from 'he was lost and has been found' to match the ending of the second act [192]. Bailey believes that this is deliberate. Jesus is inviting his critics to recognise the elder brother's sin as theirs and then get off their high horses, join the other sinners at the father's table and thus complete the story.

Jesus is a great leveller of human status since he sees all of us as equally in need of God. It makes no difference to him who shares his table. His reputation might suffer but his self-esteem remains undented whether he sits with tarts or vicars.

Aesop was right, we can discover a great deal about Jesus by the company he keeps but we can draw different conclusions from those of the Pharisees and Scribes. We observe someone who loves without fear, who is undaunted by another's record or reputation (good or bad), who values a diverse group of friends and who withholds traditional judgments. In short we find someone who never fails to see-the-human.

---

[189] Luke 15:2b.

[190] Luke 15:3-32.

[191] Chapter 7, 'Exegesis of Luke 15' in *Poet and Peasant* by Kenneth E. Bailey (Eerdmanns 1976).

[192] Compare Luke 15:24 with 15:32.

Alongside us

Being overly-fixated on reputation spawns many diseases; a healthy regard for self can slip into narcissism, a ready eye for the behaviour of others might degenerate into gossip, where we fall for the delusion that besmirching another somehow enhances our own standing. Jesus seems better at this balancing act than most and with him alongside us as our guide, we can learn much.

I love the thought of 'peculiar honours', as in the hymn,

Let every creature rise and bring
Peculiar honours to our King;
Angels descend with songs again,
And earth repeat the loud Amen.[193]

There is no record of Jesus being fussed about the background, race, status, gender, ability or sexual orientation of any of the people he met. He readily mixed with the least lovely. If he found their honours peculiar, this mattered for nothing compared with the delight he took in them. His own reputation is never his be all and end all; it always comes as a poor second to God's call to see-the-human and to love.

A quick scan of current news stories [194] reinforces our dire need to focus less on secondary issues and instead allow Jesus to teach us to see-the-human:

- An Italian captain is being prosecuted for rescuing humans from the Mediterranean in her boat. She clearly sees-the-human when she looks at desperate drowning refugees.
- Children are being held in what are in all but name, concentration camps on the US border with Mexico.

[193] The final verse of 'Jesus Shall Reign Where'er the Sun' by Isaac Watts, 1674-1748
[194] i.e. halfway through 2019.

- Uighur Muslims are disappearing from their traditional homes in China's Xinjiang province.
- There are former residents of Grenfell Tower still waiting for proper housing, two years after the inferno. There are many more tower blocks in the UK still covered with the same flammable cladding.
- Racist, homophobic and, in particular, transphobic attacks are rising at an alarming rate.
- An educational course in Birmingham, designed to introduce children to our diverse culture has prompted an intimidating series of protests outside a school (which scare the very children supposedly at risk).[195]

We are still have much to learn about seeing-the-human in each other.

> Loving Jesus
> who sat with
> prostitutes, publicans and Pharisees,
> who shrugged
> at accusations of gluttony and drunkenness,
> draw alongside us,
> receive our peculiar honours,
> help us to manage well
> our concerns about reputation,
> and most of all
> teach us always to see-the-human. **AMEN**

---

[195] The No Outsiders Project.

Day 2: Jesus was not troubled by possessions

'Do not store up for yourselves treasures on earth,
where moth and rust consume and where thieves break
in and steal; but store up for yourselves treasures in
heaven, where neither moth nor rust consumes and
where thieves do not break in and steal. For where
your treasure is, there your heart will be also.'

Matthew 6:19-21

I almost snorted with laughter when I first saw the film, *The Name of the Rose*. My derisive amusement was misplaced. The story is a murder mystery, not a comedy. It begins with a Franciscan friar accompanied by a Benedictine novice travelling to a great conference to debate an issue deemed crucial to Christian discipleship. It was this central question that tickled me so much at the time. All the effort and earnestness was for this ... to decide whether Jesus owned his own clothes. My younger self found this utterly ridiculous.

Now I grasp better the validity of this question and see that it points to so much more than clothes. The Gospels provide the monks with no definitive answer, they contain no stories of Jesus spinning, weaving or shopping. None of the evangelists record any instance of Jesus getting stroppy because Andrew borrowed his new cloak without asking and then left it out in the rain. They make no mention of Jesus owning anything at all, which might be why the monks settled on the question of his clothes. He might not have possessed tools, livestock or household items but he certainly wore clothes.

Many great spiritual thinkers have a low view of possessions. Confucius is quoted as saying, 'Trying to satisfy one's desires with possessions is like putting out a fire with straw.'

I was reflecting on this recently as our new kitchen was being fitted. Looks-wise it is a wonder which sadly leads to dissatisfaction. Its clean, clear lines reveal the shabbiness of the old laminate flooring. Once this is ripped up and replaced we will stand back to admire and try to resist the next question, 'How long can we live with this carpet? It never looked quite so threadbare alongside the previous floor …'.

There is of course no end. Feeling dissatisfied is an essential cog in the consumerist cycle. It is followed by buying the new and discarding the old (but sometimes adequate) in the hope of reaching some nebulous point where we feel that we have enough. We never will, since the acquisition of new possessions only creates further dissatisfaction and so continues the cycle.

An obvious symptom of our problem is the growth of disposable or 'fast' fashion. Currently we buy 80 billion new items of clothing every year.[196] This is a 400 per cent rise from just twenty years ago. On average, new items are binned after just five weeks. No one is winning here, apart from a few big brands. The workers are badly paid, the planet's resources are pillaged, the buyers feel pressurised, the landfills are overburdened.

Increased availability creates new pressures to wear something different whenever a camera is near, which in practice means every moment of every day. These pressures are not applied fairly; sexism is on the rampage here. Karl Stefanovic, an Australian TV presenter wore the same blue suit every day for a year, apart from the days he had it cleaned. No one commented

[196] Livia Firth, Creative Director, Eco-Age.

because no one noticed. He did this in collusion with his co-presenter Lisa Wilkinson who receives far more letters about what she wears than about what she says. The public do not apply the same pressure to Karl. This story is symptomatic of a misogynistic twist on our possessions-related disease.[197] And it is not just clothing, it is new phones, new cars and new everything else which is sourced, packaged, branded and marketed by those who repeat the lie, that retail is therapy.

Yet another symptom of this problem is hoarding. Sufferers of hoarding disorders have recently become popular subjects for TV documentaries. The rest of us watch, smugly tutting as we congratulate ourselves, 'Goodness I thought I was bad but ...'. The sobering statistic though is that hoarding affects between 2-5 per cent of the population which for the UK means 1.2 million people.

Jesus recognises how much our sense of security is bound up with our material wealth. A rich young man comes to him with a question about eternal life, probably expecting some reassurance along the lines of, 'Hey no worries for you on that score.' His confidence is based on how well he keeps certain commandments, so he is totally unprepared for Jesus' additional requirement that he must sell all his possessions on behalf of the poor.[198] I do not take this as a universal prerequisite for salvation but more as a steer from Jesus that God's salvation can never be earned. True security is found only in God and can only be ours by God's gift. This young man is determined to earn his place by his virtuous merits, so Jesus picks the one good thing that he finds impossible. He goes away disheartened but hopefully later reflects, prays and finds the humility to receive from God with open hands ... and with his hands now open, he then discovers that his possessions are not quite so important after all.

[197] See 'Karl Stefanovic's sexism experiment' by Michael Lallo in the Sydney Morning Herald, 15 November, 2014.
[198] Mark 10:17-22.

Alongside us

We have a problem with 'stuff', with our desiring, acquiring, storing and disposing of stuff. The urge to possess more, leaves us stressed rather than happy. If we recognise this as a problem and are alarmed by its scale, surely we will welcome someone who knows a better way, drawing alongside us?

Even though we do not know whether Jesus personally owned anything, we can see that he kept a wonderfully relaxed attitude about other people's stuff. He was very good at borrowing: Simon's fishing boat when he needs a preaching platform: a bucket when he is thirsty: a donkey for his trip into Jerusalem; an Upper Room for a Passover meal; and finally a tomb (although for less time than Joseph of Arimathea imagines). It seems reasonable that he would treat with the same ease whatever personal possessions he carried.

He also lays down some stringent restrictions on his followers as he sends them out on kingdom work:

> 'Take no gold, or silver, or copper in your belts, no bag for your journey, or two tunics, or sandals, or a staff; for labourers deserve their food.'[199]

He warns us less about the physical dangers and more the spiritual dangers of hoarding. We find ourselves in a bad place when possessions take over. There are no quick fixes if our collecting reaches the level of 'disorder', but perhaps a hoarder might find Jesus' presence a help in relocating their treasure. I have a feeling that the rest of us are in equal need. Our markets are designed to sabotage our homes with a choking overload of manufactured stuff. The undoing of this system has to begin with us, in our hearts.

Occasionally a billionaire tweets an epiphany about 'stuff'

---

[199] Matthew 10:9-10.

being nothing compared with family.[200] John Lennon sat in his mansion and imagined no possessions. Jesus' conclusions might sound similar but belong to a different league. Jesus speaks not from the top of a 'secure' pile of wealth, but from a position of complete dependence on God.

Jesus illustrates with a parable how ultimately any claim to 'own' anything is delusional. Our shrouds have no pockets and our tombs do not come with storage lock-ups. All is a gift from God, including our very lives. Our well-stocked warehouses will be no use to us in eternity.[201]

Loving Jesus,
help us to face our issues about possessions,
deliver us from smugness at those more severely afflicted,
embolden us to resist the pressure to acquire more,
and from alongside us,
confide to us
how you were rich to God
and how you never let stuff possess you. **AMEN**

---

[200] 'I truly believe that "stuff" really does not bring happiness. Family, friends, good health and the satisfaction that comes from making a positive difference are what really matters' Richard Branson on Twitter (@richardbranson) 29 July 2019.

[201] See the parable of the Rich Fool, Luke 12:13-21.

Day 3: Jesus was not troubled by urgency and deadlines

'My little daughter is at the point of death. Come and lay your hands on her, so that she may be made well, and live.'

Mark 5:22b

A bishop once set himself the task of travelling to every parish in his diocese. He wanted to meet as many people as possible, not just from the churches but also from their wider communities. It was an incredible undertaking. As our visit was booked for December, we gave Christmas trees to local groups to decorate and bring to church.

The afternoon was timetabled to the last minute. I, in my role as the vicar, spent considerable effort ensuring everything was in place for every given moment. We even shoehorned into the programme, a visit to a local housing project. When the day arrived we could not have been better prepared: the food was ready, the schools knew when to turn up, as did the local dignitaries and the church was full of twinkling trees, each telling a different organisation's story. Even at this point I could not see the glaring flaw in my planning. I had neglected two simple facts... the Bishop likes talking to people and people like talking to the Bishop.

I watched with rising panic as he lingered, generously engaging with each person he met. All the while the clock ticked on. During the service he invited any who wished, to come forward and be anointed with oil. Just about everyone in the packed church presented themselves for his blessing ... which he did not rush.

At one point I whispered to his Chaplain,

'I really need to hurry him up!'

The Chaplain turned to me, raised an eyebrow and said,

'Good luck with that.'

'But can't you tell him to get a move on … maybe talk to less people…?'

I petered out even before the Chaplain smiled kindly at me, gently shaking his head.

In the end it was fine. We completed our programme and all were smiling. I was too, even though my nerves were scrambled.

Jesus even more than our bishop appears to move at his own sweet speed. He seems completely in charge of his own time. I do not mean that he could have run a lucrative sideline as a time management consultant, offering the seven vital tips for highly effective diarising but more that he never seems beholden to anyone else's deadline.

Take the occasion when Jairus comes to him with the urgent news that his daughter is dying.[202] On hearing this, Jesus' next step must be obvious. Surely he will heed the kind of advice that Philip Stanhope (4th Earl of Chesterfield) gives,

'Know the true value of time; snatch, seize, and enjoy every moment of it. No idleness, no laziness, no procrastination: never put off till tomorrow what you can do today.'

Jesus proceeds as if oblivious to any urgency in this situation. He procrastinates, stopping en route for a chat with an older woman who does not seem overly keen on talking to him, at least not in public. Jesus does not hurry her. He proceeds with patient calm. I cannot imagine the frustration Jairus is feeling but surely he is grinding his teeth and bouncing around inside his shoes. And then comes the worst news possible. The little girl has died. Jairus does not say,

[202] Matthew 9:18-25, Mark 5:22-43, Luke 8:41-56.

'Maybe that's because this idiot so-called healer has absolutely zero sense of urgency!'

But who could fault him if he did?

The story ends well as Jesus proceeds to the house where he declares she has not died but is only sleeping. He awakens her and restores her to her astonished parents.

This all happens in the kind of community where people talked with each other. The events of the day would be the subject of many conversations for a while yet. I wonder what the older woman thinks when she realises the significance of the time Jesus gave to her.

Jesus hardly rushes to the twelve when they are caught in a violent storm in the middle of the Sea of Galilee.[203] We do not know how long they battle the wind and waves before he reaches them, walking on the water. He delays long enough for them to fall into a considerable panic. He could easily avert this by turning up earlier but our urgency is not his.

Lazarus likewise might have some awkward questions for Jesus when he discovers how Jesus tarries for three whole days after hearing that he was at death's door. Unlike Jairus' daughter, Lazarus unequivocally dies and is buried. His sisters, Mary and Martha are certainly alive to the bizarre nature of Jesus' time management and do not withhold their criticisms.

Martha: 'Lord, if you had been here, my brother would not have died. But even now I know that God will give you whatever you ask of him.'

Mary: 'Lord, if you had been here, my brother would not have died.'[204]

The one timing issue that haunts Jesus is 'his hour'. This appears as a cloud on the horizon throughout John's Gospel, growing ever more storm-like as the narrative continues.

---

[203] Matthew 14:22-33, Mark 6:45-56, John 6:16-24.
[204] John 11:1-44 and especially verses 21-22 and 32.

- At the wedding in Cana he tells his mother his hour has not yet come.[205]
- Twice when his opponents try to arrest him they are unable, because his hour has not yet come.[206]
- During Holy Week he declares that the hour has now arrived for him to be glorified.[207]
- He prays acknowledging that the forthcoming suffering is the very hour he has come for.[208]
- As he washes his disciples' feet, he repeats that his hour has come to depart from this world.[209]
- And just before his arrest he prays again, stating that his hour has now come.[210]

So while Jesus works to his own timescale with its all too literal 'deadline', he does not get stressed by anyone else's sense of urgency.

Alongside us

Jesus' sense of timing today might be as frustrating for us as it was for Jairus, Lazarus, Mary and Martha. Our culture tells us that we should get whatever we want in an instant. Google conditions us to expect immediate answers from its vault of seemingly limitless information. With a couple of clicks and without even leaving our sofas we can download a whole new album, order our tea and book our next flights. Is it surprising we have become so impatient with any waiting? How many of us have become grumpy when our plane is delayed? We say, 'Oh great! That's all I need. We're now running a whole hour late!' about a journey that one hundred years ago, would have

---

205 John 2:4.
206 John 7:30 and John 8:20.
207 John 12:23.
208 John 12:27.
209 John 13:1.
210 John 17:1.

taken weeks or maybe months. None of this prepares us well for life with a God who can happily sleep in the stern of the boat, despite the raging storm.

Sometimes our impatient natures can be mollified with some key bits of information, perhaps the reason for the hold up or a renewed estimate of our arrival time. With God we can expect neither of these. We ask and then we wait. Occasionally we find an answer before we have properly said 'Amen' but usually we are expected to leave our requests with God and trust that God's answer will come in God's time. We cannot speed things up. We cannot chivvy God along. Our urgency is ours, not God's.

There will be times when we will have no sense of Jesus with us. We will feel lost and utterly on our own. Wherever Jesus is, we cannot see him trotting alongside us, keeping pace with our program and up to speed with the dire needs of our situation. This is where faith becomes most real. This is the time of trial from which we pray for deliverance. Our only Godwards option is to become still and trust that God is God, despite the lack of any 'timely' answer to our pleas.

When our urgency is a matter of life and death, we find it very hard to accept Jesus' different perspective. According to him, death is more a comma than a full stop. We have his word on this but all the same we feel an overwhelming need to postpone rather than embrace the fact that each of us has a time to die.

> Jesus help us to find that deeper trust
> that looks beyond the strident demands of our urgency.
> Guide us through our disappointments,
> give us all that we need for today,
> tell us how you rose above panic,
> and keep us ever mindful of how
> you confiscated death's sting. **AMEN**

Day 4: Jesus was not troubled by future catastrophes

When you hear of wars and rumours of wars, do
not be alarmed; this must take place, but the end is still
to come. For nation will rise against nation, and kingdom
against kingdom; there will be earthquakes in various places;
there will be famines. This is but the beginning of the birth
pangs.
Mark 13:7-8

Jesus, sitting on the Mount of Olives opposite the Temple, unfolds a frightening view of the future to Peter, James, John and Andrew. The odd thing is how matter of fact he is about it all. He predicts, without alarm, wars, earthquakes, famines, persecution and the appearance of a mysterious 'desolating sacrilege'. These are all to come before the Son of Man returns and God brings this world to an end.

Those of us who grew up in the 1970s and 1980s were certain how humans would destroy the world. *Threads* on the TV, Raymond Briggs' book *When the Wind Blows* and Frankie's *Two Tribes* left us in no doubt. We were wrong (probably) but while were obsessing about the mushroom cloud, we blithely continued to pump greenhouse gases into the atmosphere.[211]

What would Jesus say about the climate emergency? Can

---

[211] I do not have the space here to explain why I believe in the human induced threat to the global climate. I am convinced by the serious warnings from the majority of reputable scientists.

we take his rather blunt predictions about future catastrophes and apply these directly to our current situation? I believe we cannot.

Sadly, Christians are among those most resistant to facing up to the climate emergency. A discouraging trawl of the internet shows me a knee-jerk mistrust of science, combined with a fear of 'liberals' (who might be ahead on this one). Perhaps giving way to them on the climate emergency might permit an avalanche of other liberal views, such as equality for women, respect for trans people and marriage for same sex couples? Add to all of this the current fashion for ignoring 'experts', combined with the ease of dismissing uncomfortable news as 'fake' and we can happily retain our chosen blinkers.

The most ridiculous counter argument to the climate emergency claims Matthew 16:2-3 as its biblical basis:

> Jesus answered [the Pharisees], 'When it is evening, you say, 'It will be fair weather, for the sky is red.' And in the morning, 'It will be stormy today, for the sky is red and threatening.' You know how to interpret the appearance of the sky, but you cannot interpret the signs of the times.

The 'reasoning' runs thus. Jesus clearly says that humans cannot affect the weather; all that we can do is observe and interpret it. Therefore we cannot be responsible for the current changes and any action we take will be pointless. The stupidity here is jaw-dropping.

Even more incredibly others argue that the end of the world, whether by nuclear war or climate catastrophe is on balance a good thing as it will prompt Jesus to return.

I read the Gospels differently and find the following points extremely relevant for our times and especially the climate emergency.

1. Jesus never shies away from an inconvenient truth. He says that the truth sets us free,[212] by which I understand that we are doomed if we stick our heads in the sand whenever presented with an awkward fact.

2. Jesus makes careful plans for the future. His long walk to Jerusalem bears this out.[213] He does not live with no thought for tomorrow in blithe trust that God will somehow work out everything for him.

3   Jesus tells stories that encourage the sort of planning that averts disaster:

*   Five bridesmaids ensure they have enough oil for their lamps, whereas the five who make no such plans miss out on the feast. [214]
*   A builder with a half-finished tower gets laughed at because they did not plan their budget.[215]
*   A king avoids a humiliating defeat by checking his enemies' forces before launching his campaign.[216]

Planning for the future can be a faithful activity and not a failure to trust God.

4. Jesus attracts attention with publicity stunts. The most notable of these is the carefully staged donkey ride into Jerusalem.[217] He also preaches openly in the Temple courts.[218]

---

[212] John 8:31-32.
[213] From Luke 9:51 onwards.
[214] The parable of the Ten Bridesmaids, Matthew 25:1-12.
[215] Luke 14:28-30.
[216] Luke 14:31-32.
[217] Matthew 21:1-10, Mark 11:1-11, Luke 19:28-40, John 12:12-15.
[218] Matthew 26:56, Mark 14:49, Luke 19:37, John 7:28, 8:20.

5. Jesus is disruptive. He famously causes havoc in the Temple by overturning the money lenders' tables and setting free the sacrificial doves.[219]

6. Jesus is never violent. His great zeal for justice never leads him to assault another human.

7. Jesus always sees the humans who are most vulnerable.

8. Jesus tells his followers to wake up. Repentance requires us to reach a level of awareness that stops us in our tracks, turns us around and compels us to seek a more positive direction.

What difference would it make if the world or even the Church adopted these eight principles, rather than promoting denial, opting for silence or abrogating all responsibility onto others?

It is true Jesus did not get stressed about future catastrophes but he did plan carefully and passionately for a righteous cause. Keep calm and carry on was never his mantra; keep calm and make wise changes might be closer (if less snappy). Some might argue that the demands of the climate emergency pale next to his great mission of winning eternal salvation for all but I am less keen to separate them into opposing choices, not least because it is the poorest who are currently suffering the most.

Yes, there will be a time when God steps in to wrap up this current order but that time is of God's choosing not ours. Until then our charge still stands, we are to act as stewards of God's creation.[220] We are not privy to God's plans for the ending of this age. We know that eventually our sun will expand into a red giant which will certainly end life on Earth as we know it. This will happen in several billion years' time.

---

[219] Matthew 21:12-13, Mark 15-17, Luke 19:45-48, John 2:13-22.
[220] Genesis 1:26.

We delude ourselves if we imagine we can somehow chivvy God along between now and then by continuing with our destructive lifestyles. Besides, we live in a masterpiece. Why would vandalising the Earth be any more acceptable than leaving a Rembrandt out in the rain?

Alongside us

Loving Jesus come to us,
draw alongside us as individuals,
as local churches and
as your global Church.

Awaken us to the difficult truths of the climate emergency,
open our eyes to see those most at risk,
guide our planning
enliven our protests,
disrupt our complacency,
teach us to find allies,
keep us from stress and
deliver us from ever condoning
harm to a fellow human. **AMEN**

Day 5: Jesus was not troubled by these other common stresses

Jesus as ever defies my attempts to fit him into neat categories. I wanted a fifth topic,

'Jesus did not find _____ difficult'

but nothing quite worked. The following are my collected thoughts which I could not work into the previous four sections but are worth raising all the same.

(i) Personal injury or illness

Jesus is never ill or if he is there is no record of this.

Gloria Copeland, a Texan evangelist and preacher capitalises on this. She gained her fifteen seconds of fame by claiming on YouTube that Jesus himself is our flu jab.[221] Apparently those of us who believe in him have no business taking vaccines because on the cross he took on all our sicknesses. By his stripes we are healed. I have a nurse friend who delights in re-posting videos like these on Facebook, partly for her amusement but more out of concern at the rapid rise of anti-vaxxers in the West and the dire risks they pose to the rest of society. I love her posts but often squirm at how often stupidity arrives on my screen, wrapped up in Jesus talk.

[221] 'Gloria Copeland Talks About the Flu', Kenneth Copeland Ministries, published on YouTube, 31 Jan 2018.

The original 'Jesus talk' (better known as the four Gospels) was never intended to be a set of comprehensive biographies. Apart from the very obvious issue of his final twenty-four hours, there is no record of Jesus suffering any illness or sustaining any physical injury. We do not read of toothache, a duvet day nursing a bout of flu or even an inflamed stubbed toe. This might be a matter of reporting or possibly he was blessed with uncommonly good health.

Can he be alongside those who suffer, when he never wakes up to yet another day of chronic pain nor grows increasingly dependent on another for his basic hygiene needs? We do not read of him needing to provide long term care for a relative. There are many stories of him meeting ill people but usually he heals them rather committing to support them as part of a care-plan.

(ii) Marriage, divorce and death of a spouse

Five out of the top ten causes of stress on the Holmes-Rahe Scale [222] are related to marriage. Some argue that every Jewish male at that time must have been married, so why imagine Jesus is an exception? However there is no mention of a wife, living or deceased in any of the Gospels and I veer towards Jesus being a perpetual bachelor. Especially, given his insistence on making women visible, it seems unlikely that this highly significant woman is there all along but only in the shadows. I think it is safe to conclude that Jesus' only experience of marriage is in the lives of others and not his own.

So again we ask, can he be alongside those with marital struggles?[223]

[222] In 1967 two psychiatrists Thomas Holmes and Richard Rahe set out to study the relationship between stressful life events and serious illness. They rated forty-three causes of stress and assigned to each a rating, which became known as the Holmes Rahe Scale.

[223] Some have speculated if homosexuality the reason for his singleness? Again I do not find enough material in the Gospels to form an opinion one way or another (despite spending considerable time looking). I can however testify that whatever Jesus was, he proved himself a trustworthy companion alongside me, as I struggled with coming out.

(iii) The daily bombardment of miserable news

Somewhere in the world at any given moment, someone is being vile to someone else. Jesus knew about 'wars and rumours of wars' but he did not have access to detailed accounts of fresh horrors each day. 'Rumours of war' have been replaced with breaking news, graphic images and live video footage. We can be aware of any new outrage within moments of it being committed.

We can switch off if we want to but that feels like turning our backs and blocking our ears to the needs of others. Part of me wishes I had not gone online on Easter Sunday morning in 2019 but the better part of me feels it was important to know about the attacks on worshippers in Sri Lanka. The news certainly changed my Easter praying. Our highly-connected world enabled me to send some supportive words to a doctor friend in Batticaloa whose hospital was receiving some of the wounded.

Jesus would have heard similar stories of cruelty and tragedy but never in such large, regular and disheartening doses. Can he understand the stress of living in our news-saturated modern world?

Alongside us

How can we imagine Jesus to be alongside us, when he has no personal experience of so many of the struggles that define us? Any list we begin quickly becomes endless, so I have curtailed the following...

Jesus has no direct personal experience of:

- getting trolled on social media,
- recovering from heroin addiction,
- suffering debilitating menstrual cramps,
- growing up trans in a transphobic culture,
- living in a society where his skin is a different colour from that of the dominant majority,
- being unable to attend work through injury or disability,

- not having the means to feed his children,
- enduring a prolonged struggle with his mental health
- being elderly and infirm … and so on.

Pursuing this line to the nth degree, we would be forced to conclude he can only truly be alongside first-century Jewish males who have an intriguing birth story.

But consider how he draws alongside the woman at the well.[224] She has her own struggles, some unique to her, some shared with some others and many that Jesus cannot personally share: she is a woman, a Samaritan, she has been married more than once and she faces cultural opprobrium for living with a man outside marriage. None of these prevent Jesus from engaging well with her.

He observes her, noticing that she comes to the well alone, under the midday sun. He engages her in a conversation that begins with a request for drink of water but then rapidly expands into theology, culture, eschatology, marriage, personal history and ends with a revelation about the identity of the Messiah.

She returns home and tells anyone who will listen, 'Come and see a man who told me everything I have ever done!'[225]

By this I am guessing their conversation was far longer than our record of it. From the little we have, we see that when Jesus has something challenging to say to her, he waits until her level of engagement gives him permission to continue.

Jacob's Well has importance to Jewish, Samaritan, Christian, and Muslim people. My hope is that Jesus' conversation there with this Samaritan woman indicates his ability to see beyond his own experiences and that many more will echo the woman's words about this character who somehow knows everything about us and still draws alongside us.

[224] John 4:1-42.
[225] John 4:29.

Jesus, despite our huge differences,
despite my struggles being far from identical to yours,
help me to trust your ability to observe,
to understand,
to listen,
and to offer you my permission,
to advise, challenge and command me. **AMEN**

Days 6 and 7: Jesus was not troubled by many of the things that stress us... concluding thoughts

Jesus offers some astonishing stress-busting advice to his listeners.

> 'Therefore I tell you, do not worry about your life, what you will eat or what you will drink, or about your body, what you will wear. Is not life more than food, and the body more than clothing?' [226]

This has been often quoted to me in calming tones when I have been feeling stressed. It is excellent advice but timing and tone of voice is key. Any suspicion of smugness leaves me more anxious than ever, only now with the added sense of failure.

I know everything he says about worry is sound. Why should we waste all that effort stressing about food, drink or clothes? If God provides these in glorious abundance for the birds of the air and the flowers of the field, how can we imagine that we will be overlooked?

However anxiety often flares up in the non-cognitive part of the brain and therefore, reasoning alone can only go so far to help. This is where a reassuring tone and comforting presence come into play. We come back to the reminders given

[226] Matthew 6:25.

at the beginning of Part 5; Jesus appears in the Gospels as a warm, engaging character, radiating joy and compelling those nearby to draw closer. In his voice, warnings about worrying are less likely to cause aggravation.

I wonder what Jesus' earthly experience of anxiety is like? Does he ever struggle with worries? And if so does he try out his wisdom on himself first? Does he tell us the kind of thing he tells himself when his own mind starts spinning?

Our next chapter is dominated by his own admission of anxiety. 'I have a baptism with which to be baptised, and what stress I am under until it is completed!' [227]

Here we find Jesus openly stressed and feeling the full weight of the world's troubles. We have this from his own mouth. His worries however are not for his everyday needs but rather for the destiny that lies before him.

[227] Luke 12:50.

Jesus was not troubled by many of the things that stress us

Questions for any time of year

1. Do you have experience of Jesus helping you with stress? What did he bring to you and how did you respond?

2. Which images of Jesus strike you as truthful? Do you favour pictures that are solemn, jovial or something else?

3. Can the risen, ascended Jesus really understand struggles that Jesus of Nazareth never experienced?

4. How do you react to Jesus building a reputation that was so at odds with society's expectations?
   a. How much does your self-esteem depend on how others perceive you?
   b. Do concerns about reputation ever dissuade you from engaging with certain people?
   c. Can you identify your own 'peculiar honours' and can you appreciate those of others?

5. Have you ever wanted to chivvy Jesus along or shout at him, 'Hurry up!' How did that work out for you?

6. Can we faithfully transpose Jesus' preparation strategies to our own current situation as we face the dangers of the climate emergency?

Jesus was not troubled by many of the things that stress us

Questions for Advent

1. Jesus never got stressed about Christmas ... how can he help you if you find that you are?

2. As you look to the future, are you optimistic, pessimistic or simply able to wait and see what happens?

3. In the light of Jesus' view of possessions, how do you view the new possessions you are currently buying for others and those soon to come your way?

4. Do you yearn for Jesus' return in glory? Do you want him to hurry up? Or would you rather he delayed for a bit longer?

5. How do you think Jesus of Nazareth would have responded to our current climate emergency?
   a. Could you plan for a 'green', climate-friendly Christmas?
   b. Is there anything you can learn from him that can become a New Year's resolution?

Jesus was not troubled by many of the things that stress us

Questions for Lent

1. How would you cope with the sudden loss of reputation that comes with being accused of a crime? How do you imagine Jesus would relate to you at such a time?

2. Thinking about your possessions:
    a. What hold do your possessions have over you?
    b. Do you ever seek comfort by acquiring more?
    c. How many items are there in your home, unused and still in their shop wrappings?
    d. Do you find any joy in parting with long-held treasures?

3. How good are you with patience? What sort of conversation would you have with Jairus or Lazarus after Jesus had not shared their sense of urgency?

4. How can you keep trusting when there is no reassuring presence, no sense of Jesus alongside you?

5. In what ways can Jesus be alongside us as we awaken to the reality of the climate emergency?

PART SIX

Jesus struggled with his destiny

Introduction – Jesus struggled with his destiny

We might pray to 'loving Jesus', or 'Jesus, full of compassion' or even 'Jesu joy of man's desiring' but would we ever call upon the equally biblical 'over-stressed Jesus' or 'deeply-troubled Jesus?'

Consider the following two verses, both of which quote Jesus directly:

> 'I have a baptism with which to be baptised, and what stress I am under until it is completed!'   *Luke 12:50*

> 'Now my soul is troubled. And what should I say - 'Father, save me from this hour'? No, it is for this reason that I have come to this hour.' *John 12:27*

Jesus' stresses certainly include his family, friends, religious neighbours and the crowds, but they all revolve around this one central point, his destiny, his coming baptism, his reason for travelling to Jerusalem at the appointed time. Even when it is in the distant future, he perceives its shadow and as time passes, so its menace grows.

Day 1: Jesus struggled with his destiny when John the Baptist was killed

[John the Baptist's] disciples came and took [John's] body and
buried it; then they went and told Jesus.

Matthew 14:12

A woman looking flustered but determined marched up to my
till in WHSmiths. This was the early 1990s and I was working
in their books department in Liverpool Street Station. She
drew an illustrated children's Bible from her bag and thunked
it down on the counter. 'I bought this as a gift for my niece. I
was told it was suitable for children. It's not. It very clearly is
NOT!'

My mind started racing, wondering what on earth she
could mean. My only guess was there was something about
the crucifixion that was too raw. Sensing my confusion, she
snatched it up again and rifled through the pages until she
found what she was looking for. She whipped it around so that
I could see a picture of a man's head on a serving plate. Blood
was spilling over the rim.

In fairness it was a rather unpleasant image. My next
comment did not help, 'Um … the story of John the Baptist *is*
in the Bible…' I began.

But she cut me off. 'Well it shouldn't be!'

I gave her a refund and returned the offending volume to

the shelf. On later reflection I conceded that the illustration was not strictly necessary but I stood by my contention that the story must not be excised on grounds of taste.

The execution of John the Baptist is a wholly repugnant episode filled with the most shameful elements:

- a rich, vain, lecherous man, who makes ridiculous promises that he is too proud to withdraw
- a murderous game played between powerful people
- the brutal death of an innocent man
- a prisoner condemned without trial
- a young woman duped into complicity
- all topped off with the gruesome spectacle of a human head on a plate.

All this is distressing for Jesus on so many levels. John is his cousin and the death of a family member always produces complicated emotions. John was a widely respected religious figure, working for good in this crazy world. His death means the ending of something fruitful and positive.

Perhaps for Jesus there is yet another level. According to the three synoptic Gospels, Jesus only begins predicting his own death after John is beheaded. We do not know for certain when Jesus first glimpses his destiny. Does he question Mary and Joseph about the gift of myrrh? Does he draw his own conclusions while studying the scriptures? Does he work out that Jerusalem was the most likely place for his death, based on its historical treatment of prophets?[228] Does John's murder bring his own destiny into sharp focus or does it reveal to him for the first time, that he too would be executed?

Thomas Hardy wrote a poem called 'The Going' following the unexpected death of his wife, Emma. He writes a one-sided conversation which ends with this verse:

---

[228] Matthew 23:27, Luke 13:34.

Well, well! All's past amend,
Unchangeable. It must go.
I seem but a dead man held on end
To sink down soon ... O you could not know
That such swift fleeing
No soul foreseeing -
Not even I – would undo me so![229]

One amongst Hardy's many sorrows, was the irrefutable reality of his own approaching death, even though he went on to live for another fifteen years.

It cannot be beyond possibility that Jesus has a similar reaction to the brutal death of John and like Hardy is 'undone'. Maybe he sees not just his own mortality but also the brutality that awaits him.

Alongside us

Very few foresee their destiny as clearly as Jesus does. Most, if not all us will face the struggles of bereavement. We increasingly want our loved ones' funerals to be bright colourful celebrations of lives well lived, that is apart from another Mr Hardy, the comedian Jeremy. He said he did not want anything joyous when he goes. Instead he fantasised about the lives of his grief-stricken relatives being torn apart. He then requested that his embalmed body be bought out whenever guests came to visit.[230]

Most, if not all of us, will face the death of a loved one before we ourselves die. None of this is comfortable. Our bereavements rank as the hardest times in our lives. It would be easier if only it were straightforward misery, but grief is a

[229] Verse 6 of 'The Going' by Thomas Hardy. I am grateful to Mark Oakley whose book *The Splash of Words* (Canterbury Press, 2016) introduced me to this poem.
[230] From the BBC Radio show *Jeremy Hardy Speaks to the Nation*, quoted in the *Independent* by Alex Nelson, 3 February 2019.

multitude of conflicting emotions that buffet and overwhelm us in no predictable pattern, taunting us with deceptive lulls in which we imagine we are moving forwards.

A dear friend in severe grief likens each new day to a cup of soup which she must drink. Every morning she finds a miserable crust of fat covering the surface. The rules dictate that she cannot discard this layer. Her only way to proceed is to pierce it and stir the grisly lumps into the rest of her day.

The artist L. S. Lowry faced an overwhelming sense of desolation after his mother died. He buried himself in his work.

'It was the only thing I had to do. I worked to get rid of the time, even now I work for something to do. Painting is a wonderful way of getting rid of the days.'[231]

No two bereavements will ever be the same. This uniqueness enhances our loneliness as we grieve. Some well-meaning people will assure us, 'I know *exactly* what you're going through.' But they do not and often this is said as a precursor to them re-visiting their own stories of loss.

Sometimes I am tempted to chime in with, 'Oh I felt kind of like that after my dear dog died,' but so far I have resisted, since those who have never loved a pet are likely to feel insulted by the comparison.

As we struggle in the face of bereavement it is good to have One alongside us who knows this struggle intimately. We thought earlier about how Jesus sought solitude to pray after John died. He defers his needs out of compassion for a hungry crowd and perhaps cut his prayers short to rescue his beleaguered twelve from the Galilean storm,[232] but nevertheless he clearly requires some personal time on the day he first hears the awful news.

[231] L. S. Lowry, 1887-1976.
[232] Matthew 14:13-32.

Jesus does not take our grief away. There is no 'opt out' for bereavement. It is a process we go undergo. Jesus' offer is to draw alongside us as we grieve, to help us in ways beyond our asking or imagining. At times, we might have no sense of his company. Maybe it will only be with hindsight that we realise he never once left us to face this struggle alone.

Jesus just be with us when we grieve,
and let us know that you're not that far away,
and even as our boat pitches, twists, turns and dives
in the storm of grief,
stay close by,
awake or asleep
on board or walking alongside
we need your presence. **AMEN**

Day 2: Jesus struggled with his destiny as he predicts his coming death

He lived among the tombs; and no one could restrain
him any more, even with a chain… Night and day among the
tombs and on the mountains he was always howling
and bruising himself with stones.
Mark 5:3 & 5

Jesus knows the fate that awaits him. He has already seen
something like it only in a reversed parallel. At the start of
his public ministry he encounters an outcast, whose enforced
situation has some uncanny similarities with the one that Jesus
willingly enters towards the end of Holy Week.

This man lives as a scorned outsider among the tombs, far
away from civilised people. He is often naked and from time to
time people come and attempt to restrain him with chains. His
torment is so intense that he self-harms. He believes that God
will only bring him further miseries. He holds within himself
enough screaming disorders to send an entire herd of pigs
over a cliff. He is considered cursed and given the mocking
name 'Legion'.

Jesus frees this man from this living hell, but later chooses
to walk calmly into his own version of the same. He is taken
outside the city to the place of the skull. He is stripped naked.
He is restrained, by nails not chains. He is tormented by many

mocking voices and angry questions about the God who has brought him to this miserable point. On the cross the very act of breathing forces him to harm himself as he pulls himself up on the nails, grating his tattered back against the rough wood.

For the man called 'Legion' release means a return to civilisation, clothed and in his right mind. Jesus will return as well, calm and clothed but not until the third day. But from the cross, his only way forward is death.

Later on different people will say different things about him. Some will say that in his dying, he held within himself the collected evils of thousands upon thousands of humans. Others will dismiss him saying, 'Cursed is everyone who hangs on a tree'.[233]

Christians can debate how much Jesus knows in advance about the exact details of his death. In each of the synoptic Gospels he predicts his death three times and his third prediction is the most detailed.[234] Matthew alone cites crucifixion as the means of death and this only once. In every other case Jesus says only that he will 'be killed'.

He knows for certain that when his death comes it will be inflicted by others and even then, only after he has been betrayed, mocked, scourged and spat upon. We should not be surprised that this knowledge brings him a great deal of stress and we return to his words in Luke:

'I have a baptism with which to be baptised, and what stress I am under until it is completed!'[235]

Can we divide his fears? Is he less stressed about the actual ending of his earthly life and more so about the humiliations

[233] Deuteronomy 21:23 and Galatians 3:13b.
[234] 1st time Matthew 16:21-23, Mark 8:31-33, Luke 9:21-2. 2nd time Matthew 17:22-23, Mark 9:30-32 Luke 9:43-45. 3rd time Matthew 20:7-19, Mark 10:32-34, Luke 18:31-34; see also John 12:23-28.
[235] Luke 12:50.

that will precede this? I have heard several people saying, 'I'm not worried about death itself, it's more the dying bit that bothers me.'

In this regard, Jesus has more to fear than most, but does that completely eclipse the aching fear of stepping into the unknown?

Towards the end of his final meal Jesus predicts his death with more than words. He breaks bread and pours out wine, telling his followers to remember him, not just by storing his words in their minds but by physically ingesting his story, his poured-out blood and his broken body. His dying is to become part of our daily routines, our sustenance and our living. This is extremely disconcerting for those around the table, who even at this late stage maintain a substantial denial around all of his predictions. Maybe during the following weeks and months, the memory of his words alongside this ritual, grow in significance as they understand more and more how Jesus who died is once again alongside them.

Alongside us

We struggle to accept our mortality. At one level, we know we all will die on day but this remains a difficult truth to fully grasp. The HBO series *Six Feet Under*, set in a Californian family-run funeral home, finishes after five seasons with the epitaph: 'Everything. Everyone. Everywhere. Ends.' This is uncomfortable but irrefutable, at least in earthly terms.

Apart from the one piece of certain knowledge (that we will all die) we have very little further information about this incredibly important event. Most of us hope we will die peacefully and without pain in our own beds, at a grand old age and surrounded by loving relatives. We have absolutely no way of guaranteeing this.

Søren Kierkegaard once quipped that, 'Life can only be understood backwards; but it must be lived forwards.' By this I think he means that our most important moments come unexpectedly and before we are fully prepared for them. The most glaring of these is our death. It would certainly help with planning if we knew more about it beforehand. Also we might make a better job of living now; there is nothing like a deadline to motivate us to get on with what matters and discard whatever does not. However this luxury is not available to us. We might live to make our century, we might get hit tomorrow by the proverbial number 57 bus. We just do not know.

We are different from Jesus in that our dying need not prompt fears of torture and humiliation. We might dread hospitals, surgeries, drips and catheters but as long as we have our NHS and our hospices, we can expect kindness and dignity. All the same we cannot avoid the fact that one day we will be gone. There will be Christmases when we buy no presents and birthday parties without us. Certain jobs we have always done will be taken on by someone else. For a while we will be remembered and then, as life rolls on, we will be forgotten.

One of the residents in HMP Manchester once explained to me how each of us dies three times. The first is at our last breath, the second is when the last person who knew us dies and the third comes the last time anyone on earth says our name. By this logic Julius Caesar still has some way to go, whereas the servant who mended his clothes has long since departed.

Jesus offers an encouraging twist to this. It comes not in the context of death, but rather when the seventy disciples return jubilant from their mission. They recount all the wonders they have performed. Jesus joins their celebrations and then caps all their achievements by saying, 'Nevertheless, do not rejoice at this, that the spirits submit to you, but rejoice that your names are written in heaven.' [236]

We will have our third death on earth but not in heaven

[236] Luke 10:20.

where our names are permanently known. As we struggle to accept our mortality this might temper some of our fears.

> Loving Jesus,
> You knew your dying would not be dignified.
> Please stay alongside us;
> we too dread humiliation,
> we fear the loss of control,
> we mourn for the life that will go on without us,
> and we wish to be included, if only in memory.
> And most of all,
> we thank you that along with our names,
> you will never forget us. **AMEN**

Day 3: Jesus struggled with his destiny in Gethsemane

'In his anguish he prayed more earnestly, and his sweat became like great drops of blood falling down on the ground.'

Luke 22:44

I spent some considerable time with a man who repeatedly stated his intention to end his life. He was in prison and at that curious stage in between being convicted and sentenced. He told me how he dreaded getting twenty years. He was not denying his crime or attempting to reduce its seriousness, in fact he barely mentioned it. His focus was fixed entirely on his future. His lawyer had warned him to expect twenty and he repeatedly told me he would not handle this. As his final day in court approached, his fears expanded rendering him unable to talk about anything apart from his impending suicide. He was relocated to the hospital wing and watched constantly.

I continued to visit him there and saw him on the morning following his sentencing. He had been given life with a recommendation to serve a minimum of twenty years before any consideration of parole. To my utter amazement, he appeared calm. His worst nightmare was now his reality but instead of going to pieces, he seemed to be coping with equanimity. His reasoning was,

'Well now I know for certain, so there's no point in worrying about it anymore. I know what I've got, so I'm just going to crack on with it.'

The *undecided* future (despite its inevitability) caused him far more stress than the *actual* future, once spelled out. He is not alone in this experience. The American aviator, Amelia Earhart is widely quoted as saying, 'The most difficult thing is the decision to act, the rest is merely tenacity.'

We can see something similar in Gethsemane. Jesus is more stressed at this moment than at any other in his earthly life. In all the horrors that later follow he appears calmer, fulfilling Isaiah's prophecy about a lamb being silent before its slaughter,[237] but in the garden, he is in such intense anguish that his sweat appears like drops of blood. There is a rare phenomenon called hematidrosis where the capillaries that feed the sweats glands rupture, staining the sweat with blood. This only happens in those experiencing the most extreme stress, such as a convict awaiting execution.

Jesus' stress is not confined solely to his forthcoming trial and crucifixion, at this moment he is still at a crossroads. He still has a choice. He could steal away into the night, reappearing months later in Egypt again as a refugee. Every part of him that dreads pains tells him that he must go … NOW! Go on *MOVE!* Whether he has any so detailed a plan is unclear. Perhaps the fight/flight/freeze section of his brain does not pause to consider disguises and possible routes to the nearest border. More likely it simply klaxons, 'GO! GO! *GO!* Get away from this place.'

The Dutch psychiatrist Bessel Van Der Kolk describes the amygdala as the brain's smoke detector, permanently on the lookout for any threats to our survival.[238] It is located in

---

[237] Isaiah 53:7.
[238] Chapter 4, 'Running For Your Life: The Anatomy Of Survival' in *The Body Keeps The Score*, Bessel Van Der Kolk (Penguin, 2014).

a more primal section than the rational part, the prefrontal cortex which he calls the watchtower. When all is running smoothly the two areas work in a complementary way; the amygdala responds to possible danger with a rush of stress hormones and the prefrontal cortex evaluates the risk and chooses an appropriate response.

In extreme danger the amygdala makes a grab for the steering wheel and tries to floor the accelerator; our primitive instinct for survival overrides our reasoning and we find ourselves moving as if pre-programmed either into fight, flight or freeze modes.

At other times there is a tug of war between the watchtower and the smoke detector as each vie for ascendancy over the other.

People with PTSD have an amygdala that once went into overload in a moment of extreme stress and now continues to 'fire off' at unexpected moments, giving them widely inappropriate reactions to non-stressful situations. The rational brain struggles against the odds to speak loudly enough to the alert sensor, like a rider trying to reason with a bolting horse.

During Jesus' long walk to Jerusalem he absorbs many threatening signs in words, warnings, arguments and hostile stares. These intensify during his final week. By this point on Thursday evening he knows exactly why Judas has slipped out. He knows too that soldiers will soon appear out of the gloom and once they do, his ending will begin. He has eyes to see. He knows how Romans terminate people.

He also knows even at this late stage, he can still step aside. His stress reaches this peak of intensity due to the simple fact that he still has a choice. We are given the privilege of eavesdropping on his most intimate prayer.

'Father, if you are willing, remove this cup from me; yet, not my will but yours be done.'[239]

[239] Luke 22:43.

This is the turning point, not the rough invasion of soldiers, not the kiss nor the arrest nor the removal into custody. This is the Rubicon moment where he makes his decision, to accept God's will over the clamour of every internal instinct screaming for self-preservation and survival.

We have seen the cracks already, the signs of this growing conflict. At Caesarea Philippi, sometime before this, Jesus blasts Peter with alarming sharpness and calling him by a new name:

> 'Get behind me, Satan! You are a stumbling-block to me; for you are setting your mind not on divine things but on human things.'[240]

Peter's crime is that he rebukes Jesus for predicting his death. Peter no doubt feels entitled to speak out, since moments before Jesus calls him 'the rock' and commends him for his astonishing level of insight into the mind of God. Now he is in trouble, for setting his mind on 'human things'. Perhaps Jesus speaks so sharply because Peter's well-meant caution blunders right into the centre of the struggle that dominates his thoughts. Perhaps Peter is giving an external human voice to Jesus' very human internal desires.

In Gethsemane we witness Jesus struggling to set his mind not on human things such as flight '*not my will*' but on divine things, '*but your will be done*'. We do not know the process by which this path was revealed to him, all we can catch is glimpses of the struggle that ensues once Jesus is convinced that God intends for him to walk this brutal way. My New Testament Greek friends tell me that from this point onwards, Mark uses only passive verbs for Jesus: now everything that happens, is done *to* him not *by* him.

Satan himself offers Jesus a short cut. Peter merely tells him that this cannot be. Satan promises him a pain-free route

[240] Matthew 16:23, Mark 8:33.

to the glorious rule of all the kingdoms of the world.[241] This surely pulls on Jesus' heart strings. It is an extremely attractive offer but the act of acknowledging Satan's authority to grant this becomes, in effect an act of worship. Human instincts such as avoiding pain, cannot be chosen at all costs. Jesus reverts to his former conviction that his call to worship God alone, must always come first.

Satan is answered with a cool quotation from the first commandment. Peter is roasted with Jesus' most fiery rebuke. Perhaps even for Jesus, injuries from a loved one cut deeper than those from an enemy.[242]

Alongside us

Many of us know the struggle of making a hard decision. We might need some quiet space to think, we might need to talk through our options with friends; both might be denied us.

This is the one time that Jesus asks his twelve (or eleven) to be alongside him as he faces his hardest decision. He needs to know that are nearby … and awake. If we can join them, if we can resist our usual distractions, we will gaze deeply into the mystery of Jesus, who is fully God and fully human, and be left with more questions than answers.

The greatness of Jesus' anguish in no way diminishes our lesser struggles but instead inspires us with confidence to trust him, since he truly understands the extremities of stress, when making pivotal decisions with dire consequences. In his unique situation, he acknowledges a call even higher than the imperative for self-preservation and when the time is right, he chooses to obey. He makes the decision of the mother hen, who surrenders her own life so that the chicks sheltering under her wings might survive. We pray 'keep us from the time of trial' because no one should ever desire to face such a choice.

[241] Matthew 4:8-10, Luke 4:6-8.
[242] See Psalm 55:12-14.

Jesus, you ask us to stay with you
and we would,
until we discover
we can only do this,
if you will stay with us.

In times of great stress,
when we are faced with appalling decisions,
when we see our own death approaching,
be alongside us
and above all other clamour,
help us to hear
God's still small voice of calm. **AMEN**

Day 4: Jesus struggled with his destiny to his dying breath

'Then Jesus gave a loud cry and breathed his last'
Mark 15:37

Finally we come to the hours when Jesus struggles physically with death. Crucifixion is an utterly barbaric way of ending someone's life. Jesus dies not through loss of blood but lack of breath. Nailed to the cross he is slumped forwards, his body pinched so that he cannot breathe. To take each next breath he must raise himself up to free his chest. His only purchase points are the nails in his wrists and feet, so pushing raw bone onto jagged iron, he lifts himself and snatches another lungfull. His final struggle is a three-hour fight for breath, where each gasp costs more than the last and each release risks the sickening jolt as his downward slump is arrested only by the nails.

> 'We may not know, we cannot tell,
> What pains He had to bear.' [243]

Many theologians since have speculated about these last hours, pondering how his suffering might incorporate the sins of all humanity but at a very human level it comes down to this; Jesus was struggling for breath, he was fighting for life.

[243] From verse two of 'There Is A Green Hill Far Away' by Cecil Frances Alexander (1848).

This is the inherited struggle humans share with all animals, to keep living even when the time for reprieve is surely long past. A rabbit yanks against its wire snare, a shrimp waves its antennae piteously through the gaps of a dockside packing crate, a fish flounders in its nets and chimps in vivisection labs continue to co-operate, despite the electrodes in their skulls. And so Jesus fights on, postponing the inevitable and resisting any fast-forward to the end. His death is the slow struggle of any animal caught in a trap.

Christians also struggle with his death. Some fetishize it. Any Western Art gallery will have more paintings of his hours on the cross than of his years of teaching. Others avoid the scene altogether. The remarkable mosaics of Ravenna show many moments from his life. The cross is always a bejewelled but empty wonder, speaking of victory rather than a struggle ending in capitulation.[244] In the church of Sant'Apollinare Nuovo there are thirteen panels depicting his Passion. We see Jesus denied by Peter, betrayed by Judas, tried by Pilate and even scourged by the soldiers but then, where we expect to see him nailed to the cross, we find his resurrection instead. His final struggle has been excised. The church found this last struggle, the visible defeat of the King of Glory (and the precursor of their Emperor) too shocking, so they cut straight to his victory.

We too cannot fathom the mysteries of his suffering. It is too much to take in. We struggle with the story of his death just as we struggle with the prospect of our own.

Alongside us through death and beyond

Growing up deep in rural Essex sounds more bucolic than it was. Now it seems idyllic but then it was just normal, even dull especially since I knew nothing else. The nearest chocolate was a five-mile bike ride away.

[244] Try searching online images of the magnificent apse mosaic of Sant'Apollinare in Classe.

We had a generous piece of land, larger than a normal garden. My parents decided that owning a donkey would be a good idea. If nothing else he would keep the grass down. Soon after he arrived they realised that he was lonely so they bought a second. The two conspired together in a way that one could not on his own and on one memorable occasion, a farmer phoned to say they had just been spotted gambolling across some distant field.

We found them and walked them home, taking a short cut through the churchyard, at the edge of which runs a small stream. The first donkey overcame his trepidation and trip-trapped across the narrow bridge, his hooves creating unnerving echoes on the wooden boards. The second refused to budge. Perhaps she had registered the hollow sounds and feared they would waken a troll in some ghastly rehash of the three billy goats gruff. Certainly, some strong instinct told her this bridge was not safe. We found ourselves in a jam. We thought about taking her the long way home, by road but she would not leave sight her friend. We tried to bring the first back over the bridge to join her but he also had decided that the bridge was a bad thing and refused to set hoof on it again. So we had two donkeys who would not be separated from each other on opposite sides of a bridge that neither was prepared to cross.

We finally persuaded her. Anyone who knows donkeys will know that they cannot be pulled from up front. They simply dig their hooves in. Their necks might stretch but they will not budge. Also they cannot be pushed from behind which is a risky business anyway because their hind legs are their best kickers. The only way to steer an unwilling donkey forwards is to stand just behind its head, take a firm grip of its halter and walk alongside it. This is how we eventually reunited the two of them and returned them to the safety of their newly reinforced paddock.

This story is my preferred way of thinking about death,

that great crossing from the known into what cannot yet be known. One day I will have to take this walk. I would rather not be dragged or pushed but I think I'll be able to cope if there was Someone who could draw alongside me, take me by the hand and walk with me, leading me onwards with confidence, on a far less painful version of the path he has trod before.

Jesus explains this to the twelve saying,

'Do not let your hearts be troubled. Believe in God, believe also in me. In my Father's house there are many dwelling-places. If it were not so, would I have told you that I go to prepare a place for you? And if I go and prepare a place for you, I will come again and will take you to myself, so that where I am, there you may be also.'[245]

We have this assurance that when our time comes, he will come to us and he will walk alongside us across the bridge and all the way to his Father's house.

Jesus you know death far more intimately than I do.
I'm not sure quite how, but I accept that;
your agony,
your struggle for breath,
your eventual collapse,
somehow opened a way through
the wall that cannot be scaled.
And I trust that,
when my time comes,
I will find you there,
and that you will walk alongside me. **AMEN.**

[245] John 14:1-3.

Day 5: Did Jesus struggle with faith in God?

'Believe me that I am in the Father and the
Father is in me.'
John 14:11

If ever a human had a great relationship with God it was Jesus. When Christians want to see what perfect faith looks like, we look to the wandering prophet from Nazareth.

His first recorded words reveal how, even at the age of twelve he believes in God as Abba, as his Father. He knows that he can draw close with the trust of a child. He strikes the perfect balance between reverence and familiarity and invites his disciples to learn this as he teaches them to pray,

> Our Father in heaven,
> hallowed be your name.[246]

He hears God's voice, affirming him as God's own son. This happens on at least three separate occasions. At his baptism God repeats,

> 'This is my Son, the Beloved, with whom I am well pleased.'[247]

---

[246] Matthew 6:9.
[247] Matthew 3:19, see also Mark 1:11 and Luke 3:22. According to John, John the Baptist witnesses not a voice from heaven, but the Holy Spirit descending on Jesus like a dove (John 1:32).

At his transfiguration, God speaks from an overshadowing cloud and says,

> 'This is my Son, the Beloved; with him I am well pleased; listen to him!'[248]

And later in Jerusalem as he approaches his death, he prays publicly for the glorifying of God's name and a voice from heaven replies, 'I have glorified it, and I will glorify it again'. [249]

Everyone there heard something. Some thought it was just a rumble of thunder but Jesus and his disciples heard the clear annunciation of words. And given these great verbal assurances, what further confirmation could Jesus possibly require?

Jesus has an enviable confidence in God. He can walk up to strangers and offer them healing, knowing he will not raise their hopes only to dash them by failing to deliver. The Spirit of God guides and prompts him in all things. How else does he trust:

* that a picnic would feed a multitude,
* that the water would be walkable,
* that the little girl is only sleeping,
* that Lazarus would hear his voice from inside the tomb,
* that Judas would betray and Peter deny,
* that death would not be the end,
* that Mary would arrive with spices and
* that ultimately love would trump all else?

He has a perfect faith in God. How else can he trust his convictions so deeply?

So why are we even asking the question, 'Did Jesus struggle with his faith?'

[248] Matthew 17:5, see also Mark 9:7 and Luke 9:35.
[249] John 12:28.

Are we seeking something unresolved in with his relationship with God? For the answer we need to go back to where we started, to the wilderness. Luke describes the third temptation where the devil takes him to the highest pinnacle of the Temple and tells him to launch himself into thin air and plummet to the earth. There is no risk of death, because God will not tolerate such an ending and will *surely* deploy angels to catch him.[250]

I understand why Jesus desires for a bit of bread after forty days of hunger. I get the appeal of a short cut to power over all the world. And this business up on the Temple's highest tower? I absolutely see why *I* would want that… but Jesus… where is the appeal for *him*? If I fell and angels caught me, I would know with a certainty rendering faith redundant, that God really exists and unquestionably loves me. Of course *I* would want that. But why did *Jesus*, given his already perfect faith? Alongside these other two temptations should we deem this one less important? Is this a token effort, doomed to fail because Jesus' faith in God is already complete?

Or it is possible that perfect faith and perfect union are not the same? Was there something further from God that Jesus craved, even burned for? Was his longing such that it almost overcame him… until the memory of a simple verse returned to him and quenched the fire, 'It is said, 'Do not put the Lord your God to the test.'"[251]

I believe Jesus did struggle with his faith, because struggle is inextricably wound into the very essence of faith; struggle is in the DNA of faith – a key component without which faith is not faith. For Jesus to be human like us, he accepts human faith, he accepts *our* type of relationship with God. He surrenders perfect union for a while and does *his* best with *our* best option. In this he does better than any other human but it was still less than he craved. Being born as one

[250] Luke 4:9-12.
[251] Luke 4:12.

of us, he is also born into our life-long struggle of desiring a union with God which will not be given in this age. So even with all the heavenly affirmations there was something still lacking, some hunger, something as yet unfulfilled ... something that might be satisfied by surrendering to this temptation ... and jumping.

Turning to St Paul's terms,[252] can it be that the incarnation rendered Jesus able to see only as through a dark glass dimly? Did he have to content himself, for the time being, to know only in part, to accept our state of yearning for more and to join us in our struggle to believe in that which we cannot see? We hope that in the next life, that we too will finally realise that perfect union with God, from which Jesus allowed himself to be distanced.

Jesus' acceptance of our lesser relationship with God is all part of the inestimable sacrifice he makes for us. It begins with his incarnation and finds its nadir on the cross, where Jesus yells out the unthinkable words, *'Eloi, Eloi, lama sabachthani?'* which means, 'My God, my God, why have you forsaken me?' (Mark 15:34)

Not that he loses faith but maybe he reaches the outer limits of human faith ... and then passes beyond. After this he is in freefall, plummeting far further than if he had jumped from the pinnacle of the Temple. He was tempted to imagine a fall that would not result in death. Instead he falls into death more deeply than any other human, before or since. And he finds that beneath all else ... love persists. And love then raises him higher than our wildest dreams.

And now, when our time comes, he will walk with us, alongside us through the tear he has rent in the very fabric of death and onwards, into a new existence, into our own perfect union with God.

---

[252] 1 Corinthians 13:12-13.

Alongside us

Anyone of us claiming to have a perfect faith in God is clearly a beginner or is heading for a fall. Those who boast about their faith have yet to grasp the implicit struggle.

Jesus responds better to the self-aware than to the brash. 'Lord I believe, help my unbelief' [253] is a far better prayer than anything beginning, 'God, I thank you that I am not like other people …'.[254]

Those who hunger, who seek, who ask and knock on the door fare better than those too well-fed to bother with looking any further. Those who have never struggled and have never felt a gnawing yearning for more, have yet to learn the true meaning of faith.

Faith is a struggle and struggle is integral to faith. We wrestle with questions, despite knowing that there are no ready answers.

- How can an all-powerful God watch the world's cruelties and not intervene?
- Why does God allow any lying buffoon to remain in office?
- How long will God wait for us to hear the cries of the poor, resisting the urge to step in personally and bring them justice?
- How can God take my loved one whilst granting health to so many who I deem less worthy?
- Where was God at *my* crucial moment?
- Why does God feel absent when most needed?

Mercifully in all our struggles, we have One who will walk with us, One who understands faith and One who knows life from both sides, from inside and out. He both *knows* the way and *is* the way… through life, through death and into everlasting life.

[253] Mark 9:24.
[254] Luke 18:11.

Loving Jesus,
as we struggle with faith,
as we yearn for more,
as we curse the dimness of our eyes
and the waywardness of our feet
as we lurch on,
finding ourselves in yet another dangerous valley
be our Good Shepherd,
guide us to the path you created long ago,
protect us from the crevices,
whose siren voices entice us
and bring us to the feast
where enmity becomes redundant
and we are fully sated less by food,
and more by your presence, alongside us. **AMEN**

Days 6 and 7: Concluding thoughts

There are two alternatives below, one for use at Christmas, and one for use at Easter. If you are reading at another time of year, either – or both – can be used.

For Advent reading: Alongside us at Christmas

'My soul magnifies the Lord, and my spirit rejoices in God my Saviour' *Luke 1:46-47*

'Look, the virgin shall conceive and bear a son, and they shall name him 'Emmanuel', which means, 'God is with us.' *Matthew 1:23*

Beyond all the excitement, beyond the demands of the kitchen, the crazy mishmash of Yule, Christian tradition, Saturnalia and Santa Claus, the daunting standards of previous years, the rushing to church (or the regrets of having stayed up too late after a midnight service) … beyond all and around all at Christmas, there is hope.

On the first day we might struggle to find this hope; the 25th of December usually arrives overladen. For some it might be too frantic to afford a single moment for reflection, for others it might be too lonely to risk any prolonged quiet, where wandering thoughts might stray to sad memories. The good news is that the whole of Christmas need not be squeezed into its first twenty-four hours; we have twelve days to celebrate our great hope.

Maybe as we watch this new baby, we should feel daunted, knowing as we do, the struggles that lie before him. Instead, our hearts are filled with wonder. We glimpse in his tiny infant form, a hope surpassing all other hopes.

We imagine Mary temporarily calming his earliest struggles with soothing words and swaddling bands until he lies at peace in her arms. Who can read her mind during these first days? She is no doubt exhausted and perhaps relieved to be still alive; in those days, many more women died in childbirth than today (speaking at least for the West.) I wonder how long after giving birth, she remembers her expectant song of hope, the Magnificat? [255]

Nine months before, as she accepts God's invitation, she sings, seeing her pregnancy as an integral part of God's new activity, affecting the whole world. The very presence of her, as yet unborn, child determines so conclusively the fate of all humanity, that Mary sings using the past tense for her future hope. Already the powerful have been dethroned, the lowly elevated, the hungry satisfied and the rich dismissed from the feast. For Mary, all of this is as good as accomplished, such is the greatness of her hope in God.

The world around Mary flatly contradicts her optimism. The poor are sorely extorted by the occupying Romans. The hungry remain empty. The powerful still call the shots. In Rome, Caesar Augustus issues a decree that forces Mary and Joseph to travel to the other end of their country. In Jerusalem, Herod shows no sign of leaving his throne; he remains secure in his brutal splendour. One of his more extravagant monuments is the Herodium near Bethlehem. He had the top of one hill removed and placed onto its neighbour. He then built a luxurious dwelling on the summit of this artificially-inflated mountain, under whose shadow, Mary and Joseph prepare for their child's arrival. The Prince of Peace is born in a poor stable, within sight of the cruel tyrant's rich palace.

[255] Luke 1:46-55.

So is Mary's optimism completely unrealistic? Does she skip too quickly to a happy ending whilst underplaying the necessary intervening struggles? History rarely tells of powerful people surrendering their thrones without quite a fight. And despite all our struggles for equality, the poor are still very much with us while the rich show no signs of leaving the high life. We have to ask, 'Are Mary's hopes too high?'

Our own hopes for this child have been modified. We have a gift of hindsight that Mary lacks; we know that Jesus did not overturn the established order and he never intended to lead a violent rebellion against the Romans. At times, some wings of the Church have viewed his revolution solely in spiritual terms, to the cost of the temporal, overplaying St Paul's instruction to struggle not against 'flesh and blood' but against 'the rulers … the authorities, [and] the cosmic powers of this present darkness.'[256] However, we cannot place all our good expectations into a box marked 'eternity' and wait resignedly until then, for all to be made well. Jesus instructs us to pray for God's will to be done on earth as it is in heaven.

Christmas tells us that God has not given up on this world. Perhaps we could use this time for rediscovering Mary's optimism for justice? Our New Year's resolutions could be bigger than some fresh personal fitness goals. Alongside our hopes for spiritual renewal, could we dare to dream of a fairer, more sustainable, less polluted world and re-structure our lives accordingly?

If we accept God's challenge to hope, we add to the struggles before us, but we do not face these alone. Jesus is named 'Emmanuel' – 'God is with us', born as one of us, born to share our human struggles. He can be invited to draw alongside us and lead us forward… with hope.

---

[256] Ephesians 6:12.

Alongside us[257]

> Be near us Lord Jesus,
> We ask you to stay,
> Alongside forever,
> And teach us the way,
> To endure and struggle,
> So God's will is done,
> On earth as in heaven,
> 'til this age has run. **Amen**

For Lent reading: Alongside us on Easter Sunday

> Sing for joy, O heavens, and exult, O earth;
> break forth, O mountains, into singing!
> For the Lord has comforted his people,
> and will have compassion on his suffering ones.
>
> *Isaiah 49:13*

Jesus' struggles become more mysterious from this point onwards. We understood him better before his death. We saw him as 'one of us', born of a woman, into the joys and constraints of human existence. As such, he shares our experience even though we now live in very different times.

But on Easter Sunday he begins a new path, one as yet untrodden by any other human. He emerges from the tomb as the first-born of God's new creation. He lives an existence in some ways recognisable to us but in so many others, far beyond our imagining. We are like goldfish seeing, through the glass wall of our bowl, a child riding a bicycle. Our piscine brains might make *some* sense of the information given through our eyes but for the most part, the child's experience is so far from our own that any theories we concoct will necessarily fall short.

We find it harder now to talk of his new struggles.

---

[257] With apologies to the original author of 'Away in a Manger'.

'Struggles' might not even be the correct word any longer. Can we still see through his eyes? Can we guess at his emotions? Can he still stub his toe? Does he ever feel stress … or pain … and is this like before or something new? He is no longer confined by locked doors.[258] He seems able to appear and disappear in ways impossible for us. Even when walking alongside us, he is able to shield our minds from recognising him, until he chooses to reveal himself in the breaking of bread.[259] We cannot track him. He used to be unpredictable, now he is completely unaccountable. He operates by rules that we cannot comprehend.

He is not a ghost but neither is he our type of human. He is still 'one of us' but is he also 'one of what we shall become'? We, like him, are born of a woman but we have no experience of being raised from the grave. We are like caterpillars meeting a moth that has successfully struggled out of its chrysalis and is now flying around us, in and out of our field of vision. We consider own earth-bound bodies and struggle to imagine how we might ever be as he is.

And there is more to this than struggling. A prize awaits the early-rising women and later the remaining fear-sodden disciples. This prize is joy - joy beyond measure. This book has been woefully short on joy. Its focus has been on Jesus' struggles. As a portrait it is necessarily skewed. Forgive me though, if I have painted Jesus of Nazareth as an overly grim-faced man, steadfastly wrestling with problem after problem throughout his thirty-three years. I attempted to balance this is Part 5 with a reminder that he is a person of radiant, compelling joy whose light attracts even those who mistrust him. His disciples may find him at time baffling but for the most part their overriding sense is of joy.

What can we say of those who lost him and now see him again? Who can estimate the quality of Easter joy spreading

[258] John 20:19.
[259] Luke 24:13-35.

among them? Who could map their thoughts as they stumble to assemble narratives to frame such dazzling splashes of wonder?

I am grateful for Thomas. He takes a bit more time, initially refusing to accept the incomprehensible. I can relate to him as one who fears being blinded; an animal transfixed by light might be caught by a new dawn or by a set of oncoming headlights. Thomas chooses to err on the side of caution. He is not present on Easter Sunday and is therefore baffled by his friends' excitement. He finds them transformed from desolate mourners into babbling idiots, united in some obscene delusion about Jesus no longer being dead. Thomas endures a whole week of this, countering their frustrated enthusiasm whilst steadfastly maintaining his conditions,

> 'Unless I see the mark of the nails in his hands, and put my finger in the mark of the nails and my hand in his side, I will not believe.'[260]

Thomas's doubts help me to understand my own.

When Jesus appears alongside him, he tells Thomas he has heard his demands and will submit to all his terms. He then instructs Thomas to reach for his hands, feet and the wound in his side. And Thomas finally accepts that this is not some bad joke but this is Jesus; the risen Jesus who is the same Jesus that died nine days ago. Thomas' story then prompts Jesus to pronounce a new privilege for the rest of us:

> 'Blessed are those who have not seen and yet have come to believe.'[261]

And this blessing is that he can be always alongside us. He can draw close to us in ways beyond our imaging and even beyond

[260] John 20:25.
[261] John 20:29b.

our perception. Unlike the original disciples, we do not need to be in any one location to be near to him. He can find us wherever we are: in a submarine in the Mariana Trench, an aeroplane high above the Gobi Desert, in a prefabricated base unit in Antarctica, an ICU, in a supermarket queue in Romford or in a prison cell in Manchester. Once he was restricted to the Holy Land and to one group of people at a time, now there is nowhere that he cannot be and no limit to the number of people within his reach.

From alongside us he does more than guide us through our struggles, he shares with us his prize at the ending of all his earthly struggles - his great prize of abiding joy.

Alongside us

If I ascend to heaven, you are there;
if I make my bed in Sheol, you are there.
If I take the wings of the morning
and settle at the farthest limits of the sea,
even there your hand shall lead me,
and your right hand shall hold me fast.
If I say, 'Surely the darkness shall cover me,
and the light around me become night',
even the darkness is not dark to you;
the night is as bright as the day,
for darkness is as light to you.[262] **AMEN**

[262] Psalm 139:8-12.

Jesus struggled with his destiny

Questions for any time of year

1. Where has Jesus featured in your times of grief?

2. What questions would you like to ask him about John the Baptist's death?

3. Can you relate to the way the disciples ignored Jesus' grim predictions? How good are you at facing uncomfortable truths head on?

4. Amelia Earhart's said: 'The most difficult thing is the decision to act, the rest is merely tenacity.'
    a. What do you make of this?
    b. How conscious are you of Jesus' presence whenever you are faced with tough choices?

5. 'We find the cross difficult, some fetishize it and others excise it.'
    a. What would a 'balanced' view look like?
    b. Is a balanced view possible?

Jesus struggled with his destiny

Questions for Advent

1. Is each child born with a destiny? (Are some born with a destiny, do some grow into a destiny, while others have a destiny thrust upon them?)

2. In your imagination, when did it dawn on Jesus that he was only relating to God by faith and that his perfect union with God had been surrendered?

3. With what mysteries do you wrestle in Advent? How good are you at living with questions or do you always *need* answers?

4. If our destiny is to face Jesus at his second coming, how do you view that?
   a. What excites you?
   b. What confuses you?
   c. Is there anything that fills you with dread?

5. How do you compare the two sacrifices, Jesus' death on the cross or Jesus surrendering his perfect union with God and accepting the limitations of human faith?

Jesus struggled with his destiny

Questions for Lent

1. At what point does Jesus realise he will die an appalling death? As a child? As a student of the scriptures? When John the Baptist dies? Or at some other moment? How does this knowledge come? In a rush, in a blinding epiphany or slowly over time, like the old TV sets warming up?

2. What assurance could God give you, that would remove all doubts from your mind?

3. Do you ever yearn for a simpler, less mysterious and more straightforward relationship with God?

4. If you could resolve just one struggle with God, which would you choose?

5. When have you found it hardest to surrender your will to God?

6. How hard must it have been to remain alongside Jesus in the garden or once he was on the cross? Think through the practical and physical ramifications as well as the emotional.

CONCLUSION

Back to Arnie and Smithy ...

We finish by returning to where we started, to a storeroom/meeting room, high up on one the wings of HMP Manchester. Arnie and Smithy are long gone but if we could meet there again, this would be my long overdue contribution to their discussion ...

So Arnie do you see? Smithy had a point all along. And yes, you were right too. Jesus *is* out there in front of us as a guiding light and a wonderful example. But he's also alongside us. He might not have gone through the whole gamut of our own individual struggles but the point is he *did* struggle. And his struggles were real, visceral and their outcome was not guaranteed. But this is good news. This means that we have even more in common with Jesus than we might have first supposed. We share these truths with him, we both know the taste of struggle, the burn, the tugging of internal fibres, as well as the cloaking power of a lie to all but completely obfuscate God's will.

> *You could always turn these stones into bread. If your Father can create the world out of nothing, this is well within your power. And who would know? It's only us here. You'd need only do a bit, just a couple of rolls to tide yourself over until you get out of this wilderness and back to civilisation.*

If this were a temptation worth talking about, Jesus would have felt a burning desire for it. A desire that grew until it seemed the most logical and practical way forward.

247

'Besides which you MUST have bread. What good will the Son of Man be if he lets himself starve to death here in the desert before he's even got properly started on God's work?'

Only there was something else, a different voice quieter and initially easier to ignore,

'Humans do not live by bread alone. That's scriptural.'

This realisation was the one that burst the all-enveloping bubble and Jesus was left staring again at a rock and wondering how it could have ever appeared as anything other.

But it was never just about bread or leaping off towers or wilderness dreams about world dominion. That insidious whisper would return to Jesus over and over. Who can tell on which other occasions the tempter appeared? After the wilderness we read,

When the devil had finished every test, he departed from him until an opportune time.[263]

And whenever that was, whatever was offered sounded right, lovely, desirable, honourable, achievable and yet... there would always be that one thing, that quiet objection which when allowed to speak deflated the fantasy.

You could MAKE your family understand you... and you know the trick. Just do it and they will be at peace. It'd be a kindness to them. They could stand alongside you, making you stronger rather than turning up at every awkward moment ... pestering you with their petty demands ... in front of everyone else too ...

You could turn the putty in your disciples' heads into something worthwhile. Actually on this one you have no choice. You simply can't leave them like this. You'll waste everything. How can you

[263] Luke 4:13.

entrust your vital 'good news' to such unreliable people? It'd be as responsible as throwing the cure for cancer to the wind. But you could force them to listen and awaken from their petty squabbles and see beyond their Galilean limits. Just imagine the future, if every time you spoke they gave you 'good soil' grade listening? Think how far that harvest would reach …

And no one is saying 'make the rich suffer' just 'make them share'. You could do that. Again, it's this much overrated free will thing. And you have authority to suspend it… I'm not saying for long, but just for a moment. With your just dominion over all, you could create the fair world which is your kingdom. And the poor would be raised up never to be crushed again. Why wait? Why leave them in the gutter for even a minute longer? Their plight is URGENT! And what will they say to you at the judgment when they finally see how you chose to prolong their misery?

And dominion over all of course includes dominion over the whole religious establishment. Stunts on a Sunday with a donkey are all well and good but come on, you've got so much more than that. You could turn the tables forever and make the whole thing work like it was always supposed to … all for the glory of your Father. You know how to proceed. Bend your opponents to your will. Switch off their objections. Why waste hours trying to reason with them when you could be spending your time teaching them as willing pupils and building a truly great future?

I know there have been hard times but there's even worse to come. So far you've got by on 'trust in God' but deep down you suspect that's not going to be enough to sustain you. It is going to get far tougher than you can imagine and it's for then, not now that you'll need proof. It's bad enough when the crowds flick between enthroning you and deserting you… Well, you don't need me to tell you how that makes you feel. But you could bear that and so much more if you were as you should be, not messing around with this flimsy faith lark that you struggle with, but living again in perfect union. I know how you can rediscover your true place. Okay, the jumping off the tower and the angels idea was a bit facile but how about …?

You see, Arnie, I'm glad that he struggled. And I'm glad that it wasn't just in the wilderness. And the fact he struggled in no sense denies his divinity, rather it demonstrates his humanity. And because he both struggled *then*, he's *now* able to draw even closer to us, to guide us, lead us and save us, not as one above, but one with us … one who truly understands our struggles.

And if we let him, he will walk alongside us.

Alongside us

> Christ be with me, Christ within me,
> Christ behind me, Christ before me,
> Christ beside me, Christ to win me,
> Christ to comfort and restore me;
> Christ beneath me, Christ above me,
> Christ in quiet, Christ in danger.
> Christ the heart of all that love me,
> Christ in mouth of friend and stranger;
> And to Him be glory forever and ever;
> and to Him be glory forever. **Amen.**[264]

---

[264] Prayer attributed to St Patrick, translated by Cecil Frances Alexander.

Appendix 1

Possible reading plan for **Advent**

Advent Sunday	Introduction: a Jesus who never struggled
First week in Advent	1. Jesus struggled with his family
Second week in Adven	2. Jesus struggled with his friends
Third week in Advent	3. Jesus struggled with religious people and structures
Fourth week in Advent	4. Jesus struggled with the crowds as the Kingdom dawned
Around Christmas Day	Alongside us at Christmas (p. 234)
First full week of Christmas	5. Jesus was NOT troubled by many of the things that stress us
The following week	6. Jesus struggled with his destiny and 7. Conclusion

Appendix 2

Possible reading plan for **Lent**

Ash Wednesday to the first Sunday in Lent	Begin with the Introduction: a Jesus who never struggled
First week of	1. Jesus struggled with his family
Second week of Lent	2. Jesus struggled with his friend
Third week of Lent and structures	3. Jesus struggled with religious people
Fourth week in Advent Lent	4. Jesus struggled with the crowds as the Kingdom dawned
Fifth week of Lent	5. Jesus was NOT troubled by many of the things that stress us
Holy Week	6. Jesus struggled with his destiny
Easter Sunday	Alongside us on Easter Sunday (p. 237) and 7. Conclusion

Acknowledgements

My thanks as ever go to my ever-loving and wonderfully supportive husband Haydn, who makes all this possible.

I am also very grateful to: Ian Fellows, Jo Calladine and Chris Fallone who read the early versions of this manuscript and offered many invaluable comments, suggestions and corrections, Professor Nihal Fernando for his psychiatric insights, the current Chaplaincy Team at HMP Manchester, for their ongoing friendship and inspiration,

Hermione Pritchard who lives in cheerful response to God's calling, Jonathan Tallon, who provided some speedy answers to some of my New Testament questions (any mistakes are mine not his), David Moloney and all the team at DLT for their continual support and encouragement.

And most of all my thanks go to my mother Anne Martin, who has filled the pages of my life's story with a consistent script of astonishing kindness. I had hoped to surprise her with the first copy of this book, which was to be dedicated to her. Instead this book is in honour of her memory. She was an inspirational woman and a wonderful mother to her three children.